God of Love and God of Reason

God of Love and God of Reason

Homilies, Lectures, and Essays on God and Religion

DAVID R. MASON

WIPF & STOCK · Eugene, Oregon

GOD OF LOVE AND GOD OF REASON
Homilies, Lectures, and Essays on God and Religion

Copyright © 2016 David R. Mason. All rights reserved. Except for brief quotations in critical publications or reviews, no part of this book may be reproduced in any manner without prior written permission from the publisher. Write: Permissions, Wipf and Stock Publishers, 199 W. 8th Ave., Suite 3, Eugene, OR 97401.

Wipf & Stock
An Imprint of Wipf and Stock Publishers
199 W. 8th Ave., Suite 3
Eugene, OR 97401

www.wipfandstock.com

PAPERBACK ISBN: 978-1-4982-2972-2
HARDCOVER ISBN: 978-1-4982-2974-6

Manufactured in the U.S.A.

For my children and their families:

Katharine Mason and her sons,
Alexander Brown and Mason Brown;

Charles Mason and his wife, Hannah Nendick-Mason,
and their children, Eleanor and Nicholas;

Thomas Mason and his wife, Julia Ridgeway-Diaz

CONTENTS

Preface | ix

Homilies

1 Jesus' Encounter with the Canaanite Woman | 3
1a Letter from a Parishioner | 7
2 Paul's Speech at the Areopagus | 13
3 Wisdom is Justified by Her Deeds | 17
4 Fundamentalism | 22
5 Evolution, Creationism, and Intelligent Design | 26
6 "God" as Depicted in Kingsley's "Water Babies" | 30
7 The Eternity and Temporality of God | 35
8 Jesus' Summary of the Law Revisited | 40
9 God: The World-Soul | 44
10 The Evolution of God | 47
11 Reason in Religion | 51
12 Moral Imagination | 56

Lectures and Essays

1 The New Atheism | 63
2 Faith in God is Not Unreasonable | 76
3 Remarks on the Atheists' Attack on Religion | 87

CONTENTS

4. Religion through My Eyes: How I Understand My Religious Beliefs and Practices | 95
5. The Roots of Antisemitism in the Gospels | 103
6. The Status of God-Talk | 111
7. Three Recent Treatments of the Ontological Argument | 119
8. Ideas and Images of God | 137
9. The Last Things: A Christian Doctrine of Hope | 150

Works Cited | 173

PREFACE

I have long been drawn to both opera and to country music because each is deeply concerned with matters of the heart. Similarly, I have long been attracted to philosophy and theology because both appeal to the head. Heart and head, love and reason, go hand in hand. In the case of God, they are "two sides of the same coin." Some time ago when I heard a recording of Gilbert and Sullivan's *H. M. S. Pinafore* and heard Josephine sing, "Oh, God of Love and God of Reason, say, which of you twain shall I obey?" I knew at once that the "twain" were not two separate and opposing deities, but that in fact the God of Love *is* the God of Reason.

The homilies, lectures, and essays that together make up this book are offered in support of this conviction: the God of Love *is* the God of Reason. And so I believe it is reasonable to have faith in a supremely loving God and that the best practices of religion are themselves reasonable. I admit that many of the so-called arguments given for belief in God have been less than fully rational: some riddled with inconsistencies; some based on faulty ideas of perfection and childish notions of power and knowledge; and some plainly irrational. I admit, too, that much of the defense of religion, especially in the modern world, has been irrational, fearful, and hateful. But worst practices and bad reasoning ought never to be taken as the standard by which the truth is measured. I think this is what both the New Atheists and Fundamentalists, in fact, do. This work is my attempt to reestablish best practices and sound reasoning so that the truth can be measured fairly.

The book has two parts: "Homilies" and "Lectures and Essays." The homilies were all preached at St. Paul's Episcopal Church in Cleveland Heights, Ohio during the first decade of the twenty-first century. They are arranged chronologically from earliest to latest. All of them are biblically grounded. At least five of the homilies (numbers 2, 6, 7, 9, and 10) are focused on the variety of ways we can reasonably understand God. Five of them (1, 3, 8, 11, and 12) are concerned with the practice of reasonable religion. And two (4 and 5) treat what I take to be unreasoning religion. Because all the homilies were written to be heard by a congregation of well-educated parishioners I believe they can be easily read and understood by generally intelligent adults, young and old.

The lectures and essays are more demanding. But they are not out of the reach of any who will take the time to read and ponder the questions. The first three were given at St. Paul's in response to the rise of the New Atheism. The fourth, "Religion through My Eyes," attempts, first, to set forth some characteristics of religion in general, and then to speak of the *theistic* religions, Judaism, Christianity, and Islam. That talk was given for a Jewish audience. The fifth talk, "The Roots of Antisemitism in the Gospels," draws together some themes I have preached about several times. The sixth, "The Status of God-Talk," was given at John Carroll University in Cleveland. The seventh is the first essay I published. I wish that the New Atheists and others were aware of the variety of careful modern treatments of the famous "Ontological Argument for the Existence of God." This essay, together with the sixth and parts of the second, tries to bring some clarity to this piece of reasoning. If the seventh was the earliest of these essays to have been written the eighth, "Ideas and Images of God," is the most recent. It was written in 2013, and given to the Pasadena Village. I am tempted to say that if readers, who might have enjoyed the homilies, get bogged down in the early essays and lectures, they should turn at once to this lecture. The last essay, "The Last Things," was published in my book, *Something That Matters*. It is my hope that publishing it here will give it a broader audience.

Many persons have graciously helped and challenged me in my thinking, preaching, and writing. I want to thank a few in particular. Years ago Donald L. Rogan urged me to go to the General Theological Seminary and has since demanded that I be reasonable and faithful. While at General I came under the influence of Norman Pittenger who introduced me to the thought of Alfred North Whitehead. When I was in graduate school at the University of Chicago my thought was shaped largely by Langdon Gilkey, David Tracy, and Schubert Ogden.

For forty years I was at John Carroll University and St. Paul's Episcopal Church in Cleveland. We raised our family in Cleveland Heights and made innumerable friends there, many connected with St. Paul's and

Preface

John Carroll, but also with University School where my wife was dean of students and psychologist. I wish to thank several rectors of St. Paul's, especially Nicholson B. White and Alan M. Gates, who allowed me to serve as "priest associate." For a year Ben Minifie was interim rector and powerfully engaged my thought. I had good conversations with many assistants, but here mention only three: Tom Culbertson, Lisa Hackney, and Richard Israel. The parishioners who befriended, supported, and challenged me are legion and, by all rights, the book ought to have been dedicated to the parishioners of St. Paul's to whom I am deeply grateful.

At John Carroll my colleagues in the Theology and Religious Studies Department were always supportive. I am especially indebted to Joseph F. Kelly, John Spencer, Paul Lauritzen, and Kathryn Merhar. I count the late Richard W. Clancey, from the English Department, a life friend and wonderful conversation partner.

In 2012 on retiring my wife and I moved to Pasadena, CA where we immediately immersed ourselves in the life of All Saints Episcopal Church and where we regularly heard brilliant preaching. We also joined the Pasadena Village, and it was for this group that I wrote and gave "Ideas and Images of God."

Lying behind nearly every page of this book are the names of three giants of philosophy and theology: Alfred North Whitehead, Charles Hartshorne, and Schubert M. Ogden. I am profoundly indebted to all three for just about everything I think, say, and write. Finally, I am, as always, deeply grateful to my wife, Margaret, for her wise and loving guidance and support. She is, as I think I have said before, the love of my life, the light of my life.

It remains to thank the editor of *The Journal of Religious Studies* for permission to reprint my article, "Three Recent Treatments of the Ontological Argument" and ABC-CLIO, the publisher of Praeger, for permission to reprint "The Last Things: A Christian Doctrine of Hope," chapter 10 of my book, *Something That Matters: A Theology for Critical Believers*.

HOMILIES

I have always found that those *Preachers* have most commanded my Heart, who most Illuminated my Head.

Benjamin Whichcote
Moral and Religious Aphorisms, #393

The power of God is the worship He inspires. That religion is strong which in its ritual and in its modes of thought evokes an apprehension of the commanding vision. The worship of God is not a rule of safety—it is an adventure of the spirit, a flight after the unattainable.

Alfred North Whitehead
Science and the Modern World, 268–69

1

JESUS' ENCOUNTER WITH THE CANAANITE WOMAN

David R. Mason
St. Paul's Episcopal Church
Cleveland Heights, Ohio
August 18, 2002

Matt 15:21–28:

> Jesus left that place and went to the district of Tyre and Sidon. Just then a Canaanite woman from that region started shouting, "Have mercy on me, Lord, Son of David; my daughter is tormented by a demon." But he did not answer her at all. And his disciples came and urged him, saying, "Send her away, for she keeps shouting after us." He answered, "I was sent only to the lost sheep of the house of Israel." But she came and knelt before him, saying, "Lord, help me." He answered, "It is not fair to take the children's food and throw it to the dogs." She said, "Yes, Lord, yet even the dogs eat the crumbs that fall from their masters' table." Then Jesus answered her, "Woman, great is your faith! Let it be done for you as you wish." And her daughter was healed instantly.

The story of Jesus and the Canaanite woman, as reported by both Matthew and Mark, is highly instructive at several levels. At the very human level we witness a woman who is desperate for the well-being of her daughter, and who discerned some sort of divine power in Jesus to help, and who persisted in pleading her case, and who, frankly, was very clever in turning a rebuff to her own advantage. Also, at the very human level we see a young itinerant Jewish teacher and healer who, just before he had come to the district of Tyre and Sidon, had been engaged with the scribes and Pharisees over the strict observance of purity laws versus the weightier matters of the Law. And one might have expected that Jesus would be here to extend the graciousness of the Jewish God and religion to the Gentiles—to make available to all sorts and conditions, irrespective of their tribal or ethnic roots, the power and salvation that he knew to be available from the personal God of the whole universe, the One whom the Jews worshiped as Yahweh and whom Jesus knew intimately as Father. As John Miller wrote: "Jesus never intended to establish a separate religion known as Christianity. Instead, He meant to extend Judaism to the whole world to welcome all Gentiles into a saving knowledge of the grace and love of Yahweh whom he frequently called Father."[1]

But, surprisingly, in this foray into Gentile territory this is *not* what Jesus initially endeavors to do. In fact, when he had the opportunity to witness to God's salvific and caring love for everyone by responding to the woman's cry for mercy he turned a deaf ear: "I was sent only to the lost sheep of the house of Israel." Evidently all discussion of God, worship, doctrines of God and the precepts of human beings, about things planted by the heavenly Father and things planted by mere humans—discussions Jesus had just had with some Pharisees—was all intramural. At this point Jesus did not seem to think that any of this concerned this pushy Gentile woman.

Moreover, when she continued to persist and knelt before him, groveled, and pleaded, "Lord, help me," Jesus finally acknowledged her, only to rebuke her with what has to be one of the most insulting putdowns in Jesus' interactions with ordinary people: "It is not fair to take the children's bread and throw it to the dogs." He likened this woman to an inferior breed; he remarked contemptuously that she was a dog! I often wonder how those folks who unctuously ask, "What would Jesus do?" deal with this snide comment. It's not, of course, that I've never belittled others or said nasty or malicious things. But one hopes for better from the One we call Lord, the Messiah of God.

Fortunately, this wasn't the final word. The insult could not pierce the armor of the Canaanite woman's faith, and her riposte is a classic: "Yes, Lord, yet even the dogs eat the crumbs that fall from their master's table." She was not to be put off because she did not belong to the right group. Her faith was in God whom she divined to be present in Jesus and that was her salvation. I don't know whether it was her humility, or her pluck, or her verbal quickness, but whatever it was it brought about a radical change in

---

1. Miller, *The Irony of Christianity*, 184.

JESUS' ENCOUNTER WITH THE CANAANITE WOMAN

Jesus' attitude and in his response to her: "O woman, great is your faith! Be it done as you desire." And her daughter was healed instantly.

Here, I really think we have moved to the divine level. And I do not mean simply that a miracle of healing was performed. I mean that, faced, with the woman's faith, her persistent sense of worth, her clever and agile wit in the face of an insult, Jesus *changed his attitude* and his understanding of who is to be included in God's salvation.

As the great American psychologist and philosopher, William James, was finishing his first book *The Principles of Psychology* he wrote to his brother, Henry, that he had to forge every sentence "in the teeth of irreducible and stubborn facts."[2] It seems to me that Jesus changed his entire outlook in "the teeth of irreducible and stubborn facts," and this is nothing short of miraculous.

Do you realize how set in our ways most of us are, and how a closed mind keeps us from dealing with irreducible and stubborn facts and expanding our horizons, from seeing new and different possibilities? One can only hope, for instance, that at the present time an administration bent upon a fixed idea that Saddam Hussein must be eliminated, taken out by what it imagines would be a quick war, will listen to the irreducible and stubborn voices from our allies in Europe and the Middle East, from Republicans in the House and Senate, from advisors such as Henry Kissinger and Brent Scowcroft, and change and take a fresh look.

I have it on a certain authority—I do not know how certain—that in the seventeenth century Oliver Cromwell, the Lord Protector, addressed the General Assembly of the Church of Scotland and said: "I beseech you in the bowels of Christ think it possible that you may be mistaken."[3] In a sense this is what the quick-witted Canaanite woman was saying to Jesus: "Think it possible that *you may be mistaken*."

So, Jesus responded. He had been mistaken that the good news of God's salvation was *only* for the lost sheep of the house of Israel. It was, of course, for the lost sheep of Israel and, indeed, for the found sheep. But it was also *for everyone else* as well. When Jesus returned to Galilee from this encounter with a Gentile woman his mission was changed. And, as is often said, "the rest is history."

To be sure, the history of the *Christian* response to Jesus has been a checkered one in which the non-Jewish beneficiaries of Christ's redemptive

---

2. See Perry, *The Thought and Character of William James*, 40.
3. Cromwell, www.cromwell.argonet.co.uk.

life have often thought that they alone were the possessors of salvation, those alone whom God loves and saves. And they frequently have asserted that they alone were the arbiters of what is true. But these people have been fighting against a changed Jesus. To speak of exclusive possession of salvation is to misread the irreducible and stubborn facts and to misrepresent Christ.

As Paul says, "There is no longer Jew or Greek, there is no longer slave or free, there is no longer male and female; for all of you are one in Christ Jesus" (Gal 3:28); and again, "In that renewal there is no longer Greek and Jew, circumcised and uncircumcised, barbarian, Scythian, slave and free; but Christ is all and in all" (Col 3:11). Or, as the great African-American spiritual has it: "In Christ there is no east or west, in him no south or north; but one great fellowship of love throughout the whole wide earth."

And I want to add: "irrespective of whether or not they are Christians."

1a

Letter from a Parishioner in response to my Aug. 18, 2002 Sermon on the Canaanite Woman Together with my letter in response to the parishioner

(The parishioner's letter was originally addressed to the interim rector who replied and sent the letter to me. I have reproduced her letter *as if it were written directly to me*, but my letter in response makes it clear that there was an intermediary.)

September 5, 2002

Dear Reverend Mason,

    I have had the privilege of hearing two others of your sermons at St. Paul's and was impressed by your message. However, I am writing this letter to express my concern over your sermon of August 18, 2002. Several of your points disturbed me and I would like to bring them to your attention.
    First was your portrayal of Jesus as possessing less than godly characteristics and secondly your utilization of the gospel to politicize your own agenda by twisting God's word.
    What I heard you say was that in Matt 15:32, Jesus Christ responded in a rude and insulting manner to the Canaanite woman. You remarked that we would have hoped for better from Jesus. Nowhere did the homily refer to other occasions when Jesus challenged those seeking his healing by testing their faith. Additionally, your intonation in your voice, when quoting

HOMILIES

Jesus' response to the woman, conveyed a derogatory translation for the word dog. The actual Greek translation for the word used, *kunarion*, means "little dog," as in a household pet, not the cur on the street you implied.

Although the Scripture passage clearly states Jesus, remarking on her great faith, blessed the Canaanite woman by healing her daughter, you verbally "rewrote" Scripture teaching that Jesus should have responded to the woman with, "I give up, you were right, I was wrong." Later you emphasized Jesus "had made a mistake" regarding his initial response to her and most disturbing to me, that Christ did not understand he was to present salvation to all peoples. Instead you explained it was the Canaanite woman who caused Jesus to recognize his error and, following this encounter, he changed his ministry, "and the rest is history."

In contrast to what you said, Christ made it clear in Matthew 8 that he knew his mission. Jesus not only blesses the Roman Centurion, who in all probability was not a Jew, by healing his servant but then he states, "Many shall come from east and west and shall sit down with Abraham and Isaac and Jacob in the kingdom of heaven." It is hard to understand how this passage does not show that prior to meeting the Canaanite woman he had full intention to carry his message to other peoples.

It concerns me that as an ordained minister you state from the pulpit that Christ's words or actions embarrass you. If Jesus had shown the lack of righteous behavior and made a "mistake," how could Jesus Christ then have been the perfect sacrifice for our sins?

Your homily then took a secular political stand by noting that, just as Christ listened to the woman and rethought his actions, so too should President Bush listen to his advisors and close allies in Europe and the Middle East. Even ignoring that those close allies in the Middle East deny Christ's resurrection and divinity, and even deny the need for a savior (which makes them odd choices for a sermon in a denomination that has at least historically taught the opposite), is your analogy any more appropriate and scriptural based than the following? *Just as Christ our Lord and Savior had disciples who consistently missed the meaning of his teachings, generally provided bad advice and even abandoned him in the Garden of Gethsemane, and then denied they ever knew him, President Bush is similarly blessed with the same sort of advisors and allies today. As Christ alone knew his calling and never wavered, so too must the President act to preserve our freedom.*

Am I wrong to prefer the cross over "crossfire," at least from the pulpit?

LETTER FROM A PARISHIONER

I would appreciate your thoughts and also a clarification regarding the last statement in your sermon, as my husband and I are seeking a church home. I look forward to seeing you on Sunday.

Sincerely yours,
_____

My response:

September 18, 2002

Dear _____

Thank you for the letter of September 5, sent to the interim rector, but clearly in response to my sermon of August 18. Also, I appreciate having talked with you after services. I said then that I would write a response to you, and so I do.

You well summarized the two points that disturbed you: that I portrayed "Jesus as possessing less than godly characteristics"; and that I utilized "the gospel to politicize [my] agenda by twisting God's word."

The first accusation, I believe, contains several issues that should be addressed. First, it is not clear, but do you intend to equate the man, Jesus, simply and without remainder, with God? You should be aware that the Gospels nowhere simply equate the historical, or pre-resurrected Jesus with God. In the twentieth chapter of John the apostle Thomas exclaims *to the resurrected Jesus*, "My Lord and my God," and that is the only such hint at an equation in the Gospels; and this, of course, is addressed to the resurrected Jesus. More typical are the titles "Messiah" (or "Christ"), "Son of God," "Son of Man," and "Lord" (and "Rabbi," "Teacher," and "Master"). Many of these titles are intended to symbolize that Jesus, as received by faith, is the representation of God-for-us, but they avoid the simple equation of a man with God.

Another issue here is what constitutes "godly characteristics." Elsewhere you mention "righteous behavior" (when you seem to imply that making a mistake would be "less than righteous behavior"). It is difficult to determine what would constitute "righteous behavior," but I suspect that making a mistake would *not* constitute *un*righteous behavior. Of course, it is also difficult for me to see what this has to do with witnessing to God's redemptive love for the world as attested by Christ. What can be said is that, *as depicted by the particular story in question (Matt 15:21–28)*, Jesus—in this particular instance—first ignored a non-Jewish woman, then asserted that he "was sent only to the lost sheep of the house of Israel," then responded to her plea for help by saying that it was unfair to take the children's food "and throw it to the dogs." Then, finally, when she persisted and made what I take to be a clever, if gentle, retort, Jesus *changed his demeanor* and said, "Woman, great is your faith! Let it be done for you as you wish." Can anyone possibly deny that radical change is depicted here?

This, I believe, opens up another issue: change—did Jesus change? *Can God change?* (I think this latter question is lurking beneath the charge, especially in light of our church conversation in which, as I recall, you asked rhetorically, "How can God change if He's perfect?") First, as you pointed out to me in Matthew 8, Jesus is shown as having a "full intention to carry his message to other peoples." But in the instance in Matthew 15, initially he intends *not* to do so, but then he changes in response to the woman's faith. In fact, there is change all along in the Gospels and this is what one would expect, for, as John Henry Newman said, "to live is to change and to be perfect is to have changed often."[1]

The other issue here is: Does, or can, God change and yet be perfect? It is a grave mistake of some ancient philosophy, uncritically accepted by some theologians, to have understood "perfection" as being in all ways "complete, and so incapable of change in any respect." The model of perfection for this philosophy was something like a rock (thought wrongly to be unchangeable) or even an abstraction (e.g., "being itself," which might be changeless). A better model for perfection is a loving person, and so a being of "pure unbounded love" would be the best candidate for perfection. But to love is to respond to those loved; to be a person is to interact, and so to change. The biblical portrait of God is that of a loving person, even a loving Father, and there are many instances of divine response and change depicted in the Bible. A classic example is Jesus' understanding of

---

1. Cited in Tracy, *Blessed Rage for Order*, 178.

LETTER FROM A PARISHIONER

God responding to prayer in the Sermon on the Mount: "What man among you," he asks, "if his son asks for a loaf, will give him a stone? . . . How much more will your Father who is in heaven give good things to those who ask him?" (Matt 7:7–12). Clearly, the God of the Bible, the God whom we worship, is affected, and so changes and responds to those he loves.

Some theologians (among them St. Thomas Aquinas and John Calvin) have thought that God, being complete and so incapable of change in any respect, as they thought, must *know all future events and things as if they had already occurred* (as people say, "God knows all things ahead of time" or "from eternity"). But this too is to substitute bad logic for piety. We can surely assert that God, being perfect, knows all the past fully and all the present *and* that God knows all the possibilities that constitute the future. But that's what the future is: merely potential. God cannot know *as actual* what has not happened (and may never happen) but is merely *possible*. That would be to know falsely, and, of course, God cannot know falsely. The content of God's knowledge changes as God knows a changing world; hence, God changes.

This is part of what I was suggesting in my sermon, and I am confident that it is at one with the gospel.

Your second accusation—that I twist God's word to politicize my own agenda—seems to assume that one ought never to comment on political situations from the pulpit, or that God's word should never be allowed to shine in judgment upon political, social, or economic matters. The great prophets of Israel did just that, and in our own day preachers as various as Martin Luther King Jr. and Pat Robertson have brought God's word to bear on political matters. I hope you agree that the "separation of church and state" doctrine does not imply that religious figures should never comment on or criticize political decisions or that the "religious" and the "secular" are airtight realms that have nothing to do with one another. But you assert that I have twisted "God's word" for my own secular political agenda.

I have certainly not twisted or distorted the *words of Scripture*, and I am confident that I have not distorted the *Word of God* that shines through the words, stories, and utterances of Scripture. It is often difficult to grasp the good news that God in Christ was reconciling the world to himself and to know how that applies to particular situations. But it surely does. And, if for freedom Christ has set me free, I am free enough to be able to criticize what I take to be a disastrous, immoral policy of preemptive first strike.

My last comment in the sermon—"irrespective of whether they are Christians or not"—was meant to assert that to be "in Christ" is to be the recipient of God's salvific love, and this is for all peoples irrespective of their religious allegiance. I am quite certain, for instance, that the words of John 14:6 do *not* imply that only baptized Christians can be saved. They mean that only by walking in the way of Christ, doing the truth, and living the life of Christ are we brought to the Father. God's love, as represented to us by Jesus Christ, is thus made available to everyone. The walls of separation (exclusivist claims to salvation by particular religions, often Jewish, Christian, and Muslim) do not help.

I hope my response to your letter will be received in the spirit in which I have written it, namely, in the love of Christ.

Sincerely,
David R. Mason

2

PAUL'S SPEECH AT THE AREOPAGUS

Sixth Sunday of Easter (May 1) 2005
David R. Mason

Acts 17:22–23

Paul's famous speech to the Athenians at the Areopagus cries out for attention from present-day Christians: "Do not neglect me," I hear it say; "Read, mark, learn, and inwardly digest." And so, to that end, I will repeat significant portions of it hoping that by leaving out some I will not distort or misrepresent the whole.

> Athenians, I see how extremely religious you are in every way. For [as I] looked carefully at the objects of your worship, I found . . . an altar with the inscription, "To an unknown god." What therefore you worship as unknown, this I proclaim to you. That God who made the world and everything in it, he who is Lord of heaven and earth . . . gives to all mortals life and breath and all things. From one ancestor he made all nations to inhabit the whole earth . . . so that they would search for God and perhaps grope for him and find him—though he indeed is not far from each one of us. For "in him we live and move and have our being" as even some of your own poets have said . . . While God has overlooked the times of human ignorance, now he commands all people everywhere to repent . . . and has given assurance to all by raising [Jesus] from the dead.

I find here three or four really significant and interrelated points that are worthy of careful consideration. But lest you mutter beneath your breath, "*Three or four!* Spare us, good Lord; we'll never get out of here awake!" let me assure you that I intend to glide swiftly through several of them and concentrate mainly on one. They are:

1. The Athenians are "extremely religious" for they seem to worship an "unknown god."
2. God is not far from each of us.
3. *In God* we "live and move and have our being."
4. This is all "good news" and is decisively revealed and declared by the life, death, and resurrection of Christ.

The first point: the Athenians and, by implication, all pagans are "extremely religious" for they worship an "unknown god." Here, I take it, is the intuition that all persons are, in today's lingo, "anonymous Christians"—that is, that, irrespective of our religion or irreligion, all persons tend toward God; they "grope for him" and in some sense "find him." As Augustine said of God: "You have made us for (*toward*) yourself and our heart is restless until it rests in you."[1] If everyone has been created by God and is oriented toward God and in some sense, however vague, worships God, then all are saved. It is the task of Christians, those who live the resurrection life, to make this explicit. It is not our task to make them explicit Christians; we can let the chips fall where they may.

This is because, secondly, "God is not far from each of us." Sometimes we want to declare God's "transcendence," God's total otherness by separating God, distancing God, from all creation. The Bible does this a bit too much, and so do theologians, preachers, liturgists, and hymnodists. But the better insight is that what distinguishes God from creatures, what constitutes God's *transcendence*, is God's universal *immanence*, God's intimacy with *all* creatures. We separate ourselves from others, and that is our shortcoming. God is at the heart of all reality, and we simply cannot separate ourselves from God. As the Muslims say, "God is closer than the vein of our neck." As Christians say, "the kingdom of God is among you" and even "within you," and sometimes "right before you." Or, "God is not far from each of us."

So, thirdly, "*In him* we live and move and have our being." Here Paul, or Luke framing a speech for Paul, makes use of a Stoic image of God as the "World Soul" in whom all things cohere, in whom all things "live and

---

1. Augustine, *The Confessions of St. Augustine*, 43.

move and have their being." We are familiar with this passage in Acts, and perhaps some of us are familiar with it as used occasionally in Morning Prayer in the Collect for Guidance: "O heavenly Father, in whom we live and move and have our being: We humbly pray thee so to guide and govern us . . ." I hope that we can discern, from these uses, that the image here is more dynamic, more interactive, more personal than that as typically understood by the Stoics (or so I'm told). I'm told that in Stoic thought the "World Soul" is impersonal and the parts that make it up are static, lifeless, and without individuality. But, for Paul, God is eminently personal, and we are free individuals for whom service to one another, love of one another, is perfect freedom. So, if God is the one in whom we live and move and have our being, God is the *personal* World Soul, the personal whole of which we are all constituent parts, and we, in turn, not only interact with one another, but contribute to the life of the encompassing World Soul.

Paul had already, in First Corinthians and Romans, appealed to the metaphor of the body of Christ as one yet containing many interactive members: "For as in one body we have many members, and all the members do not have the same function, so we, though many, are one body in Christ" (Rom 12:4–5; cf. 1 Cor 12:12). This same metaphor is, in the speech at the Areopagus, made use of, only extended beyond what is ordinarily meant by "the body of Christ," the church, to refer to the entire world: the *world* is God's *body*, and God is the *soul* that encompasses the world and interacts with all the constituent cells of the body who "live and move and have [their] being" in God. As Alexander Pope said:

> "All are but parts of one stupendous Whole,
> Whose body Nature is, and God the soul."[2]

I realize that, ordinarily, if we think of soul-body interaction, we tend to say that the "soul is *in* the body." And there is a legitimate point to this. Not that the soul is *spatially* inside the physical body, but that the soul is the personal whole that each one of us is, and acts *in*, influences, all the constituent parts of the body: the cells, the experiences, the members. As we might say, the mind races through the brain cells and, thence, into all parts of the body. Yes, in this sense the soul is in the body.

But equally true, and equally important, the cells of the body, the experiences of a living, growing life, the many constituent members, are *in* the soul, which is the unified personal whole that each of us is. The parts

2. Pope, "An Essay on Man: Epistle I."

contribute to the life of the spiritual whole; they "live and move, and have their being in" and freely contribute to, the living whole, the spiritual reality that is the soul.

So the soul-body relationship, taken as an analogy for the God-world relationship, yields the insight that *God is the soul*, "the One stupendous Whole" whose body nature, or all the world, is. All are parts of, and contribute to, this encompassing, living, growing, World Soul.

Now, we might be thinking: What difference could such an idea of God as the personal, encompassing whole, the World Soul in whom we live and move and have our being, make? (Ideas should always, and in fact do always, make a difference in how we conduct our lives.) I think that, if we but turn it over in our minds, if we let the idea of God the World Soul who "is very near to each of us," and "in whom we live and move and have our being," the "unknown God" whom we were always already worshiping—if we let *this* vision take hold of us, we will see that it makes all the difference in the world.

As I have suggested it tells us that all creatures, you and I and everyone, are already oriented toward God; we restlessly move toward the center. It tells us that God the soul is intimately related to and acting in each of us. When I pray, "Almighty God unto whom all hearts are open, all desires known, and from whom no secrets are hid," I am acknowledging that I am an open book to God because God the World Soul is with and in all the parts.

And, perhaps most importantly, this tells me that you, I, we, all of us, *make a difference to God*. For good or ill, for better or worse, we make a difference to others around us, but also to God, in whom we live and move and have our being. Just as the cells contribute, not only to the well-being of other cells, but to the soul that contains them, so we, each of us, contribute to the life of God; when we are healthy we cause rejoicing in heaven; when we do ill we cause suffering in the Soul, which is God. But always we are significant because we make a difference to God.

This, I believe, is finally the good news and this I believe is decisively revealed in the life, death, and resurrection of Jesus, the world's Messiah, our Lord.

3

WISDOM IS JUSTIFIED BY HER DEEDS

July 3, 2005
St. Paul's Episcopal Church
David R. Mason

Matthew 11:16–19, 25–30:

Jesus said: But to what will I compare this generation? It is like children sitting in the marketplaces and calling to one another, "We played the flute for you, and you did not dance; we wailed, and you did not mourn." For John came neither eating, nor drinking, and they say "He has a demon"; the Son of Man came eating and drinking, and they say, "Look, a glutton and a drunkard, a friend of tax collectors and sinners!" Yet wisdom is justified by her deeds . . . At that time Jesus said, "I thank you, Father, Lord of heaven and earth,, because you have hidden these things from the wise and the intelligent, and have revealed them to infants; yes, Father, for such was your gracious will. All things have been handed over to me by my Father, and no one knows the Son except the Father, and no one knows the Father except the Son and anyone to whom the Son chooses to reveal him. Come to me, all you that are weary and are carrying heavy burdens, and I will give you rest. Take my yoke upon you , and learn from me; for I am gentle and humble in heart, and you will find rest for your souls. For my yoke is easy, and my burden is light."

In addition to passages from the Gospel, I take as texts for this Sunday before Independence Day some well-known passages from several great American patriots and only one from our Lord Jesus Christ:

HOMILIES

The first is Jefferson's well-known passage from the Declaration of Independence: "We hold these Truths to be self-evident, that all Men are created equal, that they are endowed by their Creator with certain unalienable Rights, that among these are Life, Liberty, and the Pursuit of Happiness."[1]

Secondly, the lines penned toward the end of 1776, after Washington's army had suffered one defeat after another and only three days before Washington crossed the Delaware to capture the Hessians at Trenton—the famous words of Thomas Paine: "These are the times that try men's souls. The summer soldier and the sunshine patriot will, in this crisis, shrink from the service of their country; but he that stands by it now deserves the love of man and woman."[2]

Thirdly, a line written fifteen months before the Declaration of Independence by Patrick Henry in the fiery speech whose final line is: "I know not what course others may take, but as for me, give me liberty or give me death." But I have not chosen this line because it is much too threatening, too much of the "either/or"; rather, I choose another from the speech: "I have but one lamp by which my feet are guided, and that is the lamp of experience."[3]

Lastly, the words of Jesus in today's Gospel: "Yet Wisdom is vindicated by her deeds . . . I thank you, Father, Lord of heaven and earth, because you have hidden these things from the wise and intelligent, and have revealed them to infants" (Matt 11:19, 25).

I feel so very privileged that several times in the last decade I have had the opportunity to preach on this Sunday closest to Independence Day. I am not foolish enough to suppose that anyone remembers, but I have held up not only the ideals of Jefferson in the Declaration of Independence but also the ideals of George Mason as set forth in the Virginia Declaration of Rights: "That no free government, or the blessings of liberty, can be preserved to any people but by a firm adherence to justice, moderation, temperance, frugality, and virtue and by frequent recurrence to fundamental principles" and "That religion or the duty which we owe to our Creator and the manner of discharging it, can be directed by reason and conviction, not by force or violence; and therefore, all men are equally entitled to the free exercise of religion, according to the dictates of conscience; and that it is the mutual duty of all to practice Christian forbearance, love, and charity

---

1. The Declaration of Independence.
2. Paine, "The American Crisis, December 23, 1776."
3. Henry, "Give me Liberty or give me Death," March 23, 1775.

towards each other."[4] It is an honor and a privilege to testify to the ideals that animated the American Revolution—the ideals of freedom, equality, and justice for all—as at one with the gospel proclamation.

But there is a burden and a danger attached to preaching on Independence Day. The burden is that of living up to the ideals. The danger is that fervent patriotism can easily morph into jingoism and, because noble ideals are being proclaimed from Christian pulpits, the tendency is to identify not only the ideals but particular governmental policies with the Word of God.

Jim Wallis, in *God's Politics: Why the Right Gets It Wrong and the Left Doesn't Get It*, has said: "Abraham Lincoln had it right. Our task should not be to invoke religion and the name of God by claiming God's blessing and endorsement for all our national policies and practices—saying, in effect, that God is on our side. Rather, Lincoln said, we should pray and worry earnestly whether we are on God's side."[5]

One way to break the chains of ideology that claim God's endorsement on all national policies and practices is both to hallow the ideals and to pay close attention to what is actually done. Ideals and the rhetoric of liberty are good, but deeds and the practice and experience of the ideals is what counts. As Patrick Henry said, it is the "lamp of *experience*" that ought to guide our feet. As Jesus said, it is the *deeds* that vindicate God's Wisdom.

Let me tell you a personal story, a true story, that may illustrate this. Some of you have spotted me walking up and down Fairmount Blvd. between my house on North St. James and John Carroll University, and many have hailed me by waving or honking or calling out to me. I thank you for that. It is also true, however, that what you often have seen is a man walking with head and shoulders bent in a slouch—*not an attractive picture*! I know this, because several kind, but candid, people have pointed it out to me. On one such occasion I offered a weak, unconvincing, and not wholly honest excuse: "You see, I am deep in thought as I walk."

The reply was swift and to the point: "Well, *don't just think; look up. Look around you!*"

It is breathtaking in its simplicity: do not simply be consumed in thought; look at what's really happening; take account of the facts; pay attention to the truth of deeds; let your experience be the lamp unto your feet; let right deeds vindicate wisdom.

---

4. The Virginia Declaration of Rights, Articles XV and XVI.
5. Wallis, *God's Politics*, xvi.

HOMILIES

I cannot in all honesty say that I have fully changed my behavior, but the point struck home; and I am at least aware of my shortcomings and even try, from time to time, to face the facts and to walk straight. Bad habits are hard to break (as Paul said in today's epistle, "For I do not do what I want, but I do the very thing I hate" [Rom 7:15]) and only if we become aware of them, only if we can be very honest with ourselves and penitent and look at the facts, can our deeds begin to vindicate the wisdom.

Let us apply this example as an analogy to our great nation. Of course, we must never stop thinking. We must constantly recur to fundamental principles. But we must always be unsparing in our critical analysis. We must face the facts; we must try to vindicate the fundamental principles by corrected, righteous deeds.

This great nation, whose noble birth and noble ideals we celebrate today and tomorrow, has mostly done this. General George Washington persevered and held fast the fundamental principles. But, in fact, he changed tactics when he realized his behavior was wrong. At long last he won and set our country on its path of greatness. For the most part we have been true to our fundamental principles and have practiced righteous deeds.

But it has not always been smooth sailing. There has been the need to readjust and to change course. There have been "times that try men's souls." That part of our country that I hold dear, the South whence my forbears came, persisted in slavery for decades after the importation of slaves was banned, and it required a great, traumatic, devastating war to change our course; and then more than a hundred years to face the facts of white suppression of African-Americans.

It took the nation well over one hundred years to face the facts and the consequences of treating women as noncitizens, as nonpersons. And it has taken decades after the passage of women's suffrage for women to gain full economic, social, and political status. I can recall myself being blind to the facts.

We have continued to ill-treat Native Americans, the very poor, and homosexuals. We need to recur to fundamental principles and to *practice* those ideals, to vindicate wisdom with our deeds.

And there is the war in Iraq. There is the ill-considered war that was launched with what the "Downing Street Memos" say was "fixed intelligence," the war that was thought to be conducted on the cheap, a quick strike that would hail us as "liberators," but has gotten us into a quagmire; a war that has put us at odds with much of the world, and has divided the country; a war that has taken countless Iraqi lives, over 1,700 American lives, and has sent home countless men and women with tragic, debilitating injuries; a war that brought us shameful, immoral treatment of prisoners of war at Guantanamo and Abu Ghraib.

"These are the times that try men's souls."

I do not know how to rectify (if that is the correct word) the matter. I do not think we can simply pull out of Iraq. But I am convinced that nothing good can occur until we look inward and be honest about our real motives, and then look outward and face the facts. I believe that our country is at present trudging with its head down and its shoulders slumped.

But we are a great people with noble ideals and aspirations. It is only "sunshine patriotism" to refuse to face the facts. Even so we can straighten our shoulders and lift our heads and walk in the world once again.

"God Bless America, land that I love; stand beside her, and guide her, through the night with a light from above." Let wisdom be vindicated by her deeds.

4

FUNDAMENTALISM

David R. Mason
St. Paul's Episcopal Church
August 27, 2006

It has recently occurred to me that some of our finest preachers have found and laid bare a bit of uncommon wisdom from someone in their past who is not especially famous: Alan has appealed to his grandmother; Nick used to draw upon "Miss so-and-so" his sixth grade Sunday School teacher; this past Sunday Tony Jarvis, while praising Chave McCracken, disclosed Mary Tyler's gentle and profound way of lighting up the self-awareness of the young curate; and both Bishop Hollingsworth and Rick Taft made their greatest points about Sterling Newell by reference to things he had said and done in private.

As I have reflected on this I have had a growing sense of unease, perhaps even panic, because I cannot for the life of me recall any significant piece of practical wisdom issuing from parents, grandparents, teachers, or clergy in my youth. To be sure, there may have been profound things said or done, but quite possibly *I just wasn't paying attention.*

Come to think of it, however, my father may have uttered deep wisdom one time had I only heeded him. This was the time when I called home from university to say, "Dad, I've decided to go to seminary in order to prepare for the priesthood." After a serious pause I heard from my father: "No, no, son. Don't do a thing like that!"

But wait. There's yet another incident bubbling up into consciousness out of my youth that perhaps I ought to have paid attention to. This one involves my mother. It was a summer day, and we were sitting in the living room when several people appeared at the screen door with tracts in their hands—evangelists of some sort, doubtless biblical literalists. My mother got up, cigarette in hand, and walked to the screen door. And as they began to evangelize she broke in and stunned them with: "*We don't believe in you.*" And she quietly shut the door. OK. When I picked myself up from the floor laughing, I said, "Mother, why did you say a thing like that?" And she replied, if I recall it correctly, "Well, I didn't know what to say to them, and I didn't want to get into an argument, and that just came out": "We don't believe in you."

You know, I think my mother, who, if not the greatest intellect in the world, was nevertheless enlightened and a good person and liberated from strict, oppressive religiosity, was on to something. Of course, we believe in God. And, in fact, we believe in the God decisively revealed through Jesus Christ and attested to everywhere in Scripture. And we were then, and continued to be, worshiping Christians—Episcopalians, in fact.

But she sensed that we were being confronted with biblical fundamentalism, and I think she knew that it was wrong, wrong-headed, and poisonous. And she shut the door.

Biblical fundamentalism: What is it? What does it believe? What has it done? First, let me say that I do not want to talk about Islamic fundamentalism or even about the fundamentalism associated with the extreme Orthodox Jewish rabbis. Both groups share many of the close-minded, absolutist attitudes of Christian fundamentalists, but it is the latter who are at the doorsteps, and who pose the greatest threat to our religion. Nor am I talking about "Pentecostalism," that widespread and growing movement that treasures "speaking in tongues" as a manifestation of the Spirit. Nor am I talking about all conservative, so-called "Evangelical Protestants." Many of these Evangelicals are theologically conservative, but they are rarely absolutist, and they defend their beliefs and their interpretation of Scripture with reasoned arguments.

I am talking about an inflexible attitude that insists that the Holy Scripture, taken literally, is inerrant and the absolute and only way to obtain truth about any matter under the sun. It absolutizes the relative, which H. Richard Niebuhr said is the "great source of evil in life." In this case it absolutizes a specific set of writings, the Bible, which it declares to be "God's own truth" in any and every case, but, then when confronted with the inevitable contradictions that arise, it says, "what this means is" (implying that something is not to be taken literally) or "this is a mystery" (instead of a contradiction) or "God's truth is too high for mortals" (implying that the speaker is privy to the mind of God). And the fundamentalists typically cherry-pick the Scriptures in order to denounce particular persons or groups such as historians, scientists, those who prophetically question certain governmental policies, and, yes, homosexuals. Having thus absolutized the relative, they turn around and relativize the absolute in support of their own special prejudices.

Fundamentalism often claims to have reclaimed ancient absolute truths of Christianity, but in fact it is a modern diversion. Fundamentalism, as a movement, began in the early decades of the twentieth century as a fearful reaction against the increasing use of reason and the historical method made by mainline Protestants when examining Scripture and church history. The name "fundamentalism" derives from a series of tracts published between 1910 and 1915, called *The Fundamentals*. These tracts aimed at defining Protestant doctrine clearly and narrowly and at striking down any intelligent and expansive understanding of Scripture. The most important doctrines were: (1) the direct verbal inspiration and infallibility of the Bible; (2) the doctrine of the Trinity; (3) the miraculous, literal virgin birth of Jesus, which is to say, the belief that Mary conceived Jesus solely through the agency of the Holy Spirit without the aid of any human father—and this as the crucial test for the divinity of Christ; (4) the substitutionary theory of the atonement; (5) the belief in the bodily, physical resurrection, ascension into the clouds, and the literal Second Coming of Christ on those clouds.

Now, it is not necessary for me to examine each one of these so-called "five fundamentals." But it is necessary for me to lay bare and to criticize fundamentalism as a poisonous, irreligious, and anti-human attitude—and this as a necessary first step in the proclamation of the good news that God in Christ has reconciled the world to himself, and has made all things new by setting us free from the bondage to sin, ignorance, poverty, and oppression of the spirit.

The attitude of fundamentalism is captured in its first, and defining doctrine: that the Bible is *inerrant, infallible*; that the Bible must be taken literally, word for word, as the direct verbally inspired words of God. Of course, as I say, this opened the door for innumerable contradictions to be pointed out, and subjected the Bible and Christianity to ridicule.

But this did not stop fundamentalism. It launched an assault on all fair and objective historical work that dedicated Christian biblical scholars had achieved. The Scopes Trial in 1925 was the opening salvo. John Scopes was the obvious target, but intelligent Christianity was the ultimate victim. And fundamentalism grew: state boards of education were undermined, and politicians were taken in; creationism and so-called "intelligent design" have been promoted *in the name of Christianity* and in the teeth of science. Progressive Christianity fought back (perhaps too timidly) along with fair-minded historians and objective scientists, but this allowed fundamentalism to tar mainline Christianity with the brush of secularism.

The attack on intelligence is not the worst of it. Fundamentalism—and here is the gravamen of my charge against it—is fundamentally irreligious, *unfaithful*. By making the words of Scripture to be infallible, it has given them the place of God; it has called what is merely relative "the absolute." And then by making this god and this divine activity to be something that can be weighed out and measured by pseudo-science, it has dragged its god down to the level of the natural. Biblical literalism reduced God to the ordinary—or to magic. In some particular instances, by deifying certain sentences of Genesis or of the Holiness Code in Leviticus it even opposes Jesus who would not allow the Law, which is God's servant and our helper, to dominate.

"For freedom Christ has set us free," good Christian people. "Do not submit again to a yoke of slavery." But more than that, do not passively allow fundamentalists to arrogate to themselves the name of Christianity. "Read, mark, learn, and inwardly digest" the Holy Scriptures, and then speak out against this counterfeit. To cite Ephesians "Put on the whole armor of God." Take up the "sword of the Spirit which is the Word of God." And to paraphrase this passage, put on the breastplate of intelligence, and be shod with courage and faith and love of God and of God's world. We are contending here with principalities and powers of darkness, with the spiritual hosts of wickedness. Fundamentalism stands in the place of God; it usurps the place of God; it oppresses the human spirit; it undermines and misdirects faith. Whenever and wherever you encounter fundamentalism correct it, reject it. *Shut the door.*

. . . I had almost said, "Stand up, stand up for Jesus, stand in his strength alone."

5

EVOLUTION, CREATIONISM, AND INTELLIGENT DESIGN

David R. Mason
St. Paul's, September 2, 2006

"Rational religion appeals to the direct intuition of special occasions, and to the elucidatory power of its concepts for all occasions. It arises from what is special, but it extends to what is general."

ALFRED NORTH WHITEHEAD,
RELIGION IN THE MAKING, 31.

"When Darwin or Einstein proclaim theories which modify our ideas, it is a triumph for science. We do not go about saying there is another defeat for science, because its old ideas have been abandoned. We know that another step of scientific insight has been gained. Religion will not regain its old power until it can face change in the same spirit as does science. Its principles may be eternal, but the expression of those principles requires continual development."

ALFRED NORTH WHITEHEAD,
SCIENCE AND THE MODERN WORLD, 263.

EVOLUTION, CREATIONISM, AND INTELLIGENT DESIGN

> "The presupposition of [biblical] literalism is that God is a being, acting in time and space, dwelling in a special place, affecting the course of events and being affected by them like any other being in the universe. Literalism deprives God of his ultimacy and, religiously speaking, of his majesty. It draws God down to the level of that which is not ultimate, the finite and conditional. In the last analysis it is not rational criticism of the myth which is decisive but the inner religious criticism. Faith, if it takes its symbols literally, becomes idolatrous! It calls something ultimate which is less than ultimate."
>
> PAUL TILLICH,
> *DYNAMICS OF FAITH*, 52.

> "There is grandeur in this view of life, with its several powers, having been originally breathed by the Creator into a few forms or into one; and that, whilst this planet has gone cycling on according to the fixed law of gravity, from so simple a beginning endless forms most beautiful and most wonderful have been , and are being evolved."
>
> CHARLES DARWIN,
> *THE ORIGIN OF SPECIES*, 507.

I learned about Charles Darwin and the theory of evolution by natural selection and random variations as a child in our small Episcopal Church. My church school teacher (a student at the Virginia Theological Seminary) insisted on the compatibility of evolution and belief in God, and he taught that the Bible must never be taken as a scientific textbook. He was aware that evolution, as a legitimate scientific theory explanatory of the diversity of species and the development of the human species, was in no way at odds with a legitimate belief in God the creator, God who is decisively revealed in Jesus Christ, and God the Spirit abroad in the world. To be sure, an eighth grader did not and could not have a very thorough or precise understanding of either evolution or God. But I became convinced that it was important to my spiritual growth to promote genuine scientific theory and observation as explanatory of the natural world and also to think deeply about God and religion. And I sensed the truth of what Whitehead had written (in the year of the Scopes Trial): "Religion will not regain its old power until it can face change in the same spirit as does science"[1]

Imagine my shock when, two years later in a high school biology class, the teacher said in response to my query about evolution: "Oh, David, you mustn't believe *that*! Evolution is the work of the Devil." Evidently the teacher had not moved beyond the verdict of the Scopes Trial. Evidently she was molded in her "scientific" outlook by a powerful, but I believe irrational, religious belief.

Since the time of the Scopes Trial (and before it in many instances) much mainline Christianity in our country and in Europe has embraced the theory of Evolution. But fearful people continue to promote the teaching of "creationism" or "intelligent design" as alternative *scientific* theories. Yet the 1982 case, "Rev. Bill McLean, et al. vs. the Arkansas Board of Education" determined that "'creation-science' . . . is simply not science." "The essential characteristics of science," it stated, "are: (1) It is guided by natural law; (2) It has to be explanatory by reference to natural law; (3) It is testable against the empirical world; (4) Its conclusions are tentative, i.e., are not necessarily the final word; and (5) It is falsifiable. Creation science . . . fails to meet these essential characteristics. [It] is not science because it depends upon a supernatural intervention which is not guided by natural law. It is not explanatory by reference to natural law, is not testable, and is not falsifiable."[2] It is important to see clearly that the plaintiffs in this case were *not anti-religionists*; they were mainline Protestant and Roman Catholic leaders, together with other Protestant clergy, one biology teacher, and parents. Also various Jewish groups and the Arkansas Education Association and an association of Biology Teachers were allied "organizational Plaintiffs."[3]

Much the same, I believe, has been established with respect to "Intelligent Design" in the Dover, Pennsylvania case. "Intelligent Design," if not a fig leaf for "creation-science," is one more form of the discredited "natural theology" of William Paley.

My conviction is that "creationism" and "intelligent design" not only are not science but are false religion and/or bad theology. They treat "God"

---

1. Whitehead, *Science and the Modern World*, 263.

2. See the Memorandum Opinion of Judge William R. Overton in Gilkey, *Creationism on Trial*, 283.

3. Gilkey, *Creationism on Trial*, 269.

as if God were a natural entity acting in natural ways; they treat divine activity as if it were natural efficient causality susceptible of empirical verification or falsification. This, I believe, is a species of idolatry. Moreover, the fundamentalist proponents of these theories typically squelch the human spirit of wonder and inquiry. They know nothing of that freedom "for [which} Christ has set us free" (Gal 5:1). A better, purer spirituality might begin with the concluding remarks of Darwin's *Origins of* Species: "There is grandeur in this view of life, with its several powers, having been originally breathed by the Creator into a few forms or into one; and that, whilst this planet has gone cycling on according to the fixed law of gravity, from so simple a beginning endless forms most beautiful and most wonderful have been, and are being evolved."[4]

---

4. Darwin, *The Origin of Species*, 507.

6

"GOD" AS DEPICTED IN KINGSLEY'S "WATER BABIES"

Third Sunday of Advent—December 16, 2007
David R. Mason

"Go tell John what you hear and see: the blind receive their sight, the lame walk, lepers are cleansed, the deaf hear, the dead are raised, and the poor have good news brought to them."

(MATT 11:4–5)

"I heard, ma'am, that you were always making new beasts out of old," said Tom to old Mother Carey.

"So people fancy. But I am not going to trouble myself to make things, my little dear. I sit here and make them make themselves."

There was once, for instance, a fairy who was so clever that she found out how to make butterflies . . . And she was so proud of her skill that she went flying straight off to the North Pole to boast to Mother Carey how she could make butterflies.

But Mother Carey laughed.

"Know silly child," she said, "that anyone can make things if they will take time and trouble enough; but it is not everyone who, like me, can make things make themselves."

CHARLES KINGSLEY,
THE WATER-BABIES

"GOD" AS DEPICTED IN KINGSLEY'S "WATER BABIES"

Now, what in the name of God does this little exchange from a fairy tale have to do with Jesus' report to the disciples of John: "Go and tell John what you hear and see"? Let us see. But, first let me say a word about the author of *The Water Babies*.

Charles Kingsley was an Anglican clergyman during the middle of the nineteenth century (1819–1875) and was one of the first to use the term "Anglican" for those who appeal to Scripture, tradition, reason, and spiritually-informed experience. In addition to serving his parish, and several universities, Kingsley wrote many novels and was an early advocate of Darwin's theory of evolution. He engaged in considerable religious and theological controversy, typically favoring an enlightened Christianity, taking issue with the Evangelicals on the one side and the high-church Anglo- (or Roman) Catholics on the other. He exposed the injustices suffered by the very poor, and joined with F. D. Maurice and others in promoting "Christian Socialism."

Kingsley's sentiments about both the importance of Darwin's theory of evolution and the need for social reform appear in *The Water Babies* from which I have derived the line, "Not everyone, like me, can make things make themselves." But what, perhaps, went unnoticed by early readers was a radical revision of the understanding of God expressed herein. That is my concern. To get at that let us get a quick look at the sweep of the story:

Tom, a poor chimney sweep, is abused by Mr. Grimes, his wicked master who beats him regularly and forces Tom to do the harsh dirty work with no pay. One day, in the course of his miserable work, Tom comes down the chimney into the room of a lovely "clean" maiden only to realize how very dirty he is. He knocks over the andirons, leaps out the window, flees across the meadow to a stream where he longs to be clean! Tom leaps into the water, and immediately becomes a four-inch "water-baby" with both hands and gills—this *is* a fairy-tale.

His adventures as a water baby take him to St. Brandan's Fairy Island in the sea. Tom becomes "naughty," but longs to be good, and so is led toward ultimate righteousness, ultimate redemption, and, frankly, growth into genuine human adulthood, by fairies who are *successive incarnations of God* or of *the divine*. This is what I want you to see: the various women—and it is not in significant that they *are women*—are "incarnations" or we might say "avatars" of the divine. They are in turn: an old, "Irishwoman" who both precedes Tom and follows him in his early trials;[1] "Mrs. Bedonebyasyoudid," the fairy god of tough love who stresses punishment and reward—an eye for an eye and a tooth for a tooth;[2] her kinder, gentler sister, "Mrs. Doasyouwouldbedoneby" who clearly stresses the Golden Rule—"Do unto others as you would have them do unto you," or its more positive sibling, "Love your neighbor as yourself";[3] finally, there is "Mother Carey," the god of redemption and creation, who resides at the center of "Peacepool," and who draws all of her children—all creatures—unto herself and re-creates them: "There she sits making old beasts into new all the year round." "It is not everyone who, like me, can make things make themselves."[4]

Now, if you doubt my claim that each of these fairies is an expression of the divine, I take you to the very end of the tale where Tom and Ellie—for she is the girl into whose room he descended at the first—look into the eyes of one final fairy who appears to them:

> "Attention children!" says the fairy. "Are you never going to look at me again?"
>
> "We have been looking at you all the while," they said. And so they thought they had been.
>
> "Then look at me once more," she said.
>
> They looked, and both said at once:
>
> "You are our dear Mrs. Doasyouwouldbedoneby."
>
> "No, you are good Mrs. Bedonebyasyoudid, but you are grown quite beautiful now."
>
> "To *you*," the fairy said, "but look again."
>
> "You are Mother Carey," Tom said, "But you are grown quite young again."
>
> "To *you*," the fairy said, "Look again."
>
> "You are the Irishwoman who met me with Grimes."
>
> —And when they looked she was none of them, yet all of them at once.
>
> "My name is written in my eyes, if you have eyes to see it there."
>
> And they looked into her great, deep, soft eyes, and they changed again and again into every hue as the light changes in a diamond.

1. See Kingsley, *The Water Babies*, 17.
2. Kingsley, *The Water Babies*, 63.
3. Kingsley, *The Water Babies*, 64.
4. Kingsley, *The Water Babies*, 87.

"GOD" AS DEPICTED IN KINGSLEY'S "WATER BABIES"

> "Now read my name."
> And her eyes flashed, for one moment, clear, white, blazing light; but the children could not read her name, for they were dazzled, and hid their faces in their hands![5]

So many manifestations of the One, transcendent, yet universally immanent God!

Oh, to be sure, as I have repeated, this is but a fairy tale. Yet fairy tales, like myths, like parables, like good poetry, while they ought not to be taken literally, must be taken seriously. And so I recur to the words of Mother Carey, the manifestation of God the creator and redeemer: "Know, silly child, that anyone can make things if they will take time and trouble enough; but it is not everyone who, like me, can *make things make themselves*."[6]

Think. Isn't this a profound expression of divine creativity in a world of evolving creatures? God does not simply make things "*out of nothing*" (a bad philosophical guess). God does not fashion humans out of inert matter (the dust of the ground in Genesis) much as an artisan is said to fashion pots from clay (an inadequate biblical image found throughout the Hebrew Scriptures and in Romans). No, God's creativity is much more wonderful and more powerful and more creative than these images suggest. God's creative power is at work in individuals who themselves already have a measure of freedom and power and responsibility. God makes things make themselves! This is not simply trickery or mind control or subtle coercion; there is nothing of the manipulative potter here; there is no medieval ruler with total control of feudal subjects; God is not an angry religious authority who browbeats immature souls and stifles the growth of reason, nor is God a CIA agent threatening and "waterboarding" a terrified terrorist; God is neither hypnotist nor puppeteer who directs our every move.

God creates in us the will and the ability to choose, to make decisions, small and great, to create and recreate ourselves from moment to moment in response to the creative freedom of others; God enables each of us to create ourselves and to act for good in others.

I suppose that the best clearly human example that I know that mirrors this divine creativity is that of parents who enable their children to grow slowly, but surely into independent, loving, decision-making adults. The parents do not act *for* the child; they do not eliminate options or remove obstacles. Rather, they present increasing options and try to make

---

5. Kingsley, *The Water Babies*, 10/1–/208.
6. Kingsley, *The Water Babies*, 88.

those they deem the best to be the most attractive. Thus, they enable the child to create herself.

Come to think of it, this is what good friends do, and this is what we in a community of love do with one another: we enable one another to create and recreate ourselves.

Think, finally, of Jesus of Nazareth who, for Christians, is the ultimate expression of divine love and the divine creativity in world history. Jesus did not run roughshod over the crowds or the disciples. He never coerced or manipulated; he tried to make God's rule of love as attractive as possible even though it entailed the cross. Even his so-called "miracles" should not be read in a crudely literal way as divine interventions that suspend the laws of nature or eradicate human freedom. They must be read as attractive fairy tales that enable us to see that in the midst of life's storms there is a "Peacepool" that redeems, recreates, and strengthens us.

"Go tell John what you hear and see: the blind receive their sight; the lame walk, lepers are cleansed, the deaf hear, the dead are raised, and the poor have the good news brought to them."

What is the "good news"? "Everyone who is in Christ is a new creation; the old has passed away, behold everything is new" (2 Cor 5:17); "Now the Lord is the Spirit, and where the Spirit of the Lord is, there is freedom" (2 Cor 3:17). The good news is God's love operative in the world and in our lives enabling us to accept the facts and the truth of our lives, but always to see new possibilities; to accept the fact that God desires us to be whole beings, which is what salvation and cleansing are about; to be raised up to freedom, freedom from want and freedom for justice and the good for others.

7

THE ETERNITY *AND* TEMPORALITY OF GOD

16th Sunday After Pentecost
August 31, 2008

Exodus 3:1–15:

Moses was keeping the flock of his father-in-law Jethro, the priest of Midian; he led his flock toward the wilderness, and came to Horeb, the mountain of God. There the angel of the Lord appeared to him in a flame of fire out of a bush; he looked, and the bush was blazing, yet it was not consumed. Then Moses said, "I must turn aside and look at this great sight, and see why this bush is not burned up." When the Lord saw that he had turned aside to see, God called to him out of the bush, "Moses, Moses!" And he said, 'Here I am." Then he said, ""Come no closer! Remove the sandals from your feet, for the place on which you are standing is holy ground." He said further, "I am the God of your father, the God of Abraham, the God of Isaac, and the God of Jacob." And Moses hid his face, for he was afraid to look at God.

Then the Lord said, "I have observed the misery of my people who are in Egypt; I have heard their cry on account of their taskmasters. Indeed, I know their sufferings, and I have come down to deliver them from the Egyptians, and to bring them up out of that land to a good and broad land, a land flowing with milk and honey, to the country of the Canaanites, the Hittites, the Amorites, the Perizzites, the Hivites, and the Jebusites. The cry of the Israelites has now come to me; I have also seen how the Egyptians oppress them. So come, I will send you to Pharaoh to bring my people, the Israelites, out of Egypt. But Moses said to God; "Who am I that I should go to Pharaoh, and bring the Israelites out of Egypt?" He said, "I will be with you; and this shall be the sign for you that it is I who sent you: when you have brought the people out of Egypt, you shall worship on this mountain."

But Moses said to God, "If I come to the Israelites and say to them, 'The God of your ancestors has sent me to you,' and they ask me, 'What is his name?' what shall I say to them?" God said to Moses, "I AM WHO I AM." He said further, "Thus you shall say to the Israelites, 'I AM has sent me to you.'" God also said to Moses, "Thus you shall say to the Israelites, 'The LORD (YHWH), the God of your ancestors, the God of Abraham, the God of Isaac, and the God of Jacob, has sent me to you': This is my name forever and this is my title for all generations."

The lectionary readings from Genesis and Exodus have, for the past many Sundays, put us in touch with the roots of our religion. They have called forth the legendary early ancestors, the heroes and heroines of our faith, who not only establish our heritage and go before us, but who, as the Epistle to the Hebrews says, surround us with "so great a cloud of witnesses." We have heard again of Abraham and Sarah and Hagar, of Isaac and Ishmael; we learned of Isaac and Rebekah, and of their children, Esau and Jacob, Jacob the "smooth man"; we heard of Jacob and his wives, Leah and Rachel, sisters who bore him many sons, one of the younger of whom was Joseph. Finally, we have arrived at the greatest hero of them all: Moses, the liberator, who leads the Israelites from bondage in Egypt into the wilderness to make a covenant with YHWH. Also we are introduced to Miriam, his sister, who cunningly maneuvers Pharaoh's daughter to call Moses' mother to nurse the baby Moses (for wages!); then later on we will learn that Miriam was the first to sing of the downfall and destruction of Pharaoh's army:

> "Sing to the Lord, for he has triumphed gloriously;
> Horse and rider he has thrown into the sea" (Exod 15:21).

These are all wonderful stories of perseverance, courage, and pluck; and no matter that the ancient authors tell us considerably more than we really want to know—say about Hittites, Perizzites, and Jebusites, or the many long lists of descendents of obscure people, or of the details of the Ten Plagues—we love them because they tell us of the early heroes of faith. And I suspect that one of the attractive things about these stories, one of the reasons that we return to these heroes and heroines of faith, is that most of them are flawed;

THE ETERNITY AND TEMPORALITY OF GOD

they have feet of clay. Like Peter and Paul in the New Testament, these towering figures at the beginning of the journey—Abraham and Sarah; Isaac and Rebekah; Jacob and his two wives; Joseph; Moses and Miriam—variously weave vices into their virtues. They are at times callous, stupid, cupid, and timid, devious, clueless, hotheaded, and even vindictive. We love them because they are so much like we are—and yet they have faith.

All of these stories, however, would be little better than stories of Pecos Bill or Paul Bunyan or Anne of Green Gables were it not for that towering figure who is always before, behind, and within these stories, namely, *God*, the one they often identify as YHWH.

It is God who is really the central figure of all of these stories, and it is this God who discloses himself to Moses in today's reading: the God of Abraham, the God of Isaac, the God of Jacob; this God who has heard the cry of the people in harsh slavery in Egypt and who sends Moses to confront Pharaoh and to release the people from bondage, from oppression, so that they may worship God freely on the mountain of God; it is this God who identifies himself enigmatically as "I AM WHO I AM," and says, "say 'I AM' has sent you."

There is so much about the God whom we are called to worship that is packed into this brief story that we could hardly do better than to meditate on this encounter. Of course, there is much more throughout the Bible about God that needs to be said: God as creator of all things great and small; God of the prophets who demands justice and who, nevertheless, is filled with compassion; above all, God as the Father of Jesus, the Christ—God disclosed as "pure unbounded love." Even so, let us attend to the significant traits of God as revealed by this story: God is here disclosed to be *eternal*—or immutable—on the one hand (the term often used in the tradition is "absolute"). And on the other hand, God is disclosed as affected by the cries of the Israelites in their present situation, and with a past and a future, and so *temporal* (the term often used is "relative," having relations that affect or change the being).

How can this be? Does it make sense to say that God is immutable or changeless, that God is eternal and, at the same time, insist that God has a past and an open future, and that God changes in response to the changing needs of creatures? Can we really say that God is both *absolute* and *relative*—which is to say that the absolute God also has relations with others, relations that make a real difference to God's life? Can we say that our *eternal* deity has *temporal* relations that affect and so change it? Let us see. Let us examine this passage and unpack it.

The key statement for those who insist that God is absolute and immutable or unalterable is: "I am Who I am." The present tense of the verb, "to be"—*am*—indicates utter constancy, sheer immutability or changelessness. Understood this way, God would simply not have been said to have had a past. And in no way would anyone think that God has an open future facing unactualized possibilities. Here God simply "is." I am thinking of St. Thomas Aquinas here who says that the most proper name of God is, "*He Who Is*," which signifies being solely in the present ("being itself") and knowing "not past or future."[1] But Aquinas is not alone; he reflects a broad spectrum of believers who have bought into the notion that any kind of change is bad, that to be *perfect* is to be *complete*, and so incapable of change, and that the perfect being, therefore, must know what we call "the future" as already having been completed and so simply and only the present: "I am Who I am." I am "He Who Is."

Nevertheless, this same passage also tells us that this God has a *past*: "I am the God of Abraham, of Isaac, and of Jacob." And this tells us that, although there is continuity with the past, there is also change. We learn too that God has "heard the cry" of the people in their suffering; thus God *feels*, or is affected by, the plight of the people, and so *responds* to a new and desperate situation. Moreover, God engages Moses as he is keeping the flock of his father-in-law and *sends* him both to Pharaoh and to the people. And even though the implication is that God will prevail, the outcome in its detail is by no means certain. Past, present, future; remembering, feeling for, response, anticipation: *change*.

Am I stretching the material to make a point? I don't think so, but I admit that I would need to draw upon much other biblical material to nail down the conviction that God loves, and so is affected; that God hears, feels, has compassion, and so is changed in his or her inner being; and then that God responds to particular needs; that God "risks" because God does not know the outcome of things;[2] that God is supremely *personal*. Still, the essence of all this can be seen in this story.

Therefore, we see that the story of God encountering Moses at the burning bush tells us, at one and the same time, that God is immutable, eternal, or absolute and that God changes, is temporal, or relative. Is this a contradiction, an impossibility? This is what our theological ancestors believed, and so they ignored the obvious temporality, sociality, and relativity

---

1. Aquinas, *Basic Writings of Saint Thomas Aquinas*, 131–32.
2. See Sanders, *The God Who Risks*.

THE ETERNITY AND TEMPORALITY OF GOD

of this God; they insisted that God is simply and only eternal, immutable, absolute. To be sure, in their religious life, their prayer life, they were bound to accept God as personal. But in their life of the mind—their theology—they wiped the divine slate clean of personal traits, of temporality, social relations that entail change, of risk and openness to new possibilities. We can do better. But we must learn to make important distinctions with regard to the God we worship. We need to see *what trait* or attribute applies to *what aspect* of God.

The point is this: *that* God always exists (although we do not) is unalterable (God necessarily exists; this is the deepest meaning of God as eternal or absolute); moreover, that God *inevitably loves* and wills the best for the creatures, in whatever situation they find themselves, is certain; that God knows completely, in perfect detail, *all the past* is true (but, of course, God could not know *the future* as actual, or as if it had already come about and were present, because future events *have not happened*; God cannot know what is merely possible as if it were actual). So much is eternal or immutable about God. All this is epitomized by the phrase; "I AM WHO I AM."

But the God who always exists, who inevitably wills the best, loves, and responds; the God who knows what can be known—this God changes in the content of God's life just as any person changes by virtue of interactions with others. Abstractions and ideals may remain the same; they are changeless. Real persons are affected, interact, change, grow. We know this about ourselves, and the change is not merely superficial, physical change; nor is it merely a matter of inconstancy or vacillation. To be a person is to relate, to be social, to be affected by our relationships, to love, to grow, to change.

God always exists, and on that we can rely; God always changes, and for that we can be thankful. For, God the supreme person of the universe knows and loves each of us in our particularity, and is thus affected, changed, made new each morning by what we do or do not do.

As I have often said, when singing the hymn, "Immortal, Invisible, God Only Wise," and when I get to the lines, "We blossom and flourish like leaves on the tree, then wither and perish, but *nought* changeth thee," I know that "nought changes God's *bare existence*," but sing lustily, "and *aught* changeth thee." That is to say, every little thought, gesture, deed makes a difference to and so changes God. If we are something that matters we matter to God; we make a difference not only in the world but in God. We affect God; God changes. And that makes all the difference in the world.

8

JESUS' SUMMARY OF THE LAW REVISITED

October 26, 2008
David R. Mason

Matthew 22: 34–40:

When the Pharisees heard that he had silenced the Sadducees, they gathered together, and one of them, a lawyer, asked him a question to test him. "Teacher, which commandment in the law is the greatest?" He said to him, "'You shall love the Lord your God with all your heart, and with all your soul, and with all your mind.' This is the greatest and first commandment. And a second is like it: 'You shall love your neighbor as yourself.' On these two commandments hang all the law and the prophets."

You, no doubt, noticed that I followed the Collect for Purity this morning with the Summary of the Law rather than skipping straight to the *Gloria in excelsis*. I do this from time to time, and having heard today's Gospel, perhaps you can understand why I fix on Jesus' response to the lawyer's question about which commandment in the Law is the greatest: "'You shall love the Lord your God with all your heart, and with all your soul, and with all your mind.' This is the greatest and first commandment. And a second is like it: 'You shall love your neighbor as yourself.' On these two commandments hang all the law and the prophets." You see, I believe this to be one of the most profound statements about the nature of religion, faith, worship, God, and ethics ever to have been made.

JESUS' SUMMARY OF THE LAW REVISITED

And, for that reason, I think that the statement ought to be repeated often, committed to memory, and meditated on frequently. I realize, of course, that religion is a complex phenomenon and cannot be reduced to an easily memorized slogan. I realize too that the God we worship is a many-sided being and that this suggests that God's relation to the world is complex so that, as a great philosopher once said, although we should "seek simplicity," we should likewise "distrust it."[1]

Even so, I also know that great religious geniuses, who have had plenty to say about God, religion, faith, prayer, worship, have nonetheless tried on occasion to boil it all down to a single, short insight. Rabbi Hillel, for instance, is said to have responded to the question how to formulate the essence of Judaism briefly with a negative form of the Golden Rule: "What is hateful to you do not do to your neighbor; that is the whole Torah, the rest is commentary; go and learn it."[2] And Rabbi Jesus, among his many pithy sayings in the Sermon on the Mount uttered a positive form of the Golden Rule: "In everything do to others as you would have them do to you; for this is the law and the prophets" (Matt 7:12).

Now, maybe you will agree with me that the Golden Rule, whether in its negative or positive form—do or do not do to unto others as you would have them do or not do to you—is not as sound an ethical principle as the positive Levitical saying: "*Love* your neighbor as yourself" (Lev 19:18). And so Paul, who also had many other significant things to say, said, "The whole law is summed up in a single commandment: 'You shall love your neighbor as yourself'" (Gal 5:14).

Moreover—back to Jesus in today's encounter with the Pharisees—Jesus realized that this insight was an essential part of a complex whole. But notice the order of the whole: the lawyer asked for the single greatest commandment in the Torah, and Jesus responded straight from Deuteronomy, a passage that he must have recited thousands of times as a child and young man: "You shall love the Lord your God with all your heart, and with all your soul, and with all your mind" (Deut 6:5) But he intuitively grasped the need for the ethical corollary that he found amidst the dreck of the Holiness Code in Leviticus: "You shall love your neighbor as yourself" (Lev 19:18; perhaps he should have looked closer and said, "You shall love the *alien* as yourself" [Lev 19:34]).

---

1. Whitehead, *The Concept of Nature*, 163.
2. See Steinberg, *Basic Judaism*.

I believe that the answer Jesus gave in this instance discloses his genius for getting to the heart of religion as love of God with the totality of our being, and for the ethical demand that this entails. First, however, observe that Jesus did not formulate a new insight. That is to say when asked for the greatest commandment in the Torah he went to the Torah and quoted from it in two places: Deut 6:6, which follows the *Shema*: "Hear, O Israel, the Lord our God, the Lord is One." And then he quoted from Lev 19:18: "You shall love your neighbor as yourself."

Nor, it occurs to me as surely it has occurred to others, is his order—worship of God, first, and the ethical imperative to love of neighbor and all whom God loves, second—new. The Ten Commandments, which in one of its two expressions is close to the Deuteronomy passage, puts attention to God and worship first, and then lays out ethical demands. The first four of the Ten Commandments, from "I am the Lord your God . . . You shall have no other gods before me" to "Remember the Sabbath day, and keep it holy" are about God and worship. Then the next six, from "Honor your father and your mother" to "Do not covet your neighbor's goods" are all about ethical demands. I suppose that, if you care about numbers and quantity, you might think that ethics is, here, more important than worship—six to four! Sometimes Jesus seems to agree: "Not everyone who says to me 'Lord, Lord,' will enter the kingdom of heaven, but only the one who does the will of my Father in heaven" (Matt 7:21) and "When the Son of Man comes" he will say, "Truly I tell you, just as you did it to one of the least of these my brothers and sisters you did it to me" (Matt 25).

All of this discloses the complexity of religion and its resistance to being easily simplified (And, should any of you wish to return to church at 10 or 11 this morning to hear James Carroll, I suspect you will hear something of the dark side of religion; at least in his book, *Constantine's Sword* and in the film of the same name he lays bare some of the negativities of our religion). But, in respect to order (worship and God, first; ethics, second) *and* in his emphasis upon *love* as central to both, Jesus' Summary of the Law and the Prophets has it over anything else!

Loads of people have noticed it, but it bears repeating what Paul Tillich said: the "character of genuine *faith*," which Tillich called "the state of being ultimately concerned," is put "unambiguously" in the biblical words: "You shall love the Lord your God with all your heart, and with all your soul, and with all your might."[3] And the philosopher Charles Hartshorne

---

3. Tillich, *Dynamics of Faith*, 3.

JESUS' SUMMARY OF THE LAW REVISITED

added: "To worship [any being] is to 'love' [that being] 'with all one's heart and all one's mind and all one's soul and all one's strength.' . . . The genius of Tillich," he added, "first perceived that this formula is potentially the clearest definition in religious literature of the term, 'God.'"[4]

I would have said it was the genius of *Jesus*, or of *John*, or even of various Old Testament figures, to have defined God in terms of love. But my point is: faith in God, worship of God, is primary, and that means *love* of God with the *totality* of our being; it also means that the God we love *is* the God of *love*, is the One who first loved us, for that is the essence of creation and redemption; second, love of God with all our being entails loving all God loves, all creatures great and small. And this is the lens though which we must see and articulate our ethical principles: *love*. The six ethical demands of the Ten Commandments are merely *mitzvoth* (either "commands" or "good deeds") unless they are controlled and transformed by love: "Love your neighbor as yourself" because God loves all.

Jesus said to the lawyer who asked for the greatest commandment in the Law: "You shall love the Lord your God with all your heart, and with all your soul, and with all your mind. This is the greatest and first commandment. And a second is like it: You shall love your neighbor as yourself. On these two commandments hang all the law and the prophets."

Take this with the utmost seriousness. Repeat it frequently, memorize it, meditate on it, and let it define your worship and your behavior.

Amen.

---

4. Hartshorne, *The Logic of Perfection*. 40.

9

GOD: THE WORLD-SOUL

David R. Mason, St. Paul's
Feb. 8, 2009

Rabbi Milton Steinberg tells us of a homily from ancient rabbinic literature: "It is written in the Psalms, 'Bless the Lord, O my soul.' Why did David bid his soul in particular to praise God? Because he said, 'As the soul pervades the body, God pervades the world. . . . As the soul sustains the body, God sustains the world . . . As the soul survives the body, God survives the world . . . Wherefore let the soul of the body praise Him who is, as it were, the soul of the world.'"[1]

God, as "the soul of the world"; God as the "World Soul." It is a brilliant image, I think, yet one not much used in biblical writing, nor even much in rabbinic or Christian theological writing. There are a few instances, that I will tell you about, but none, I believe, in the Bible that itself tends to think of God as separate from the world and over against it much like Michelangelo's painting in the Sistine Chapel: God is seen as creator, to be sure, but a creator from without; God is also understood to be the sustainer, leader, lord, father, spirit, etc., but one whose acts always seem to come from without and to interrupt the flow of natural and historical events (hence, miracles); God is, of course, the judge, redeemer, lover, friend; yet no matter how lovingly concerned God is, there is inevitably a distance between God and the world. There is nothing of the intimacy and intertwining that we might think a soul and its body have.

---

1. Steinberg, *Basic Judaism*, 52.

GOD: THE WORLD-SOUL

The image of God as World Soul may not replace the many important biblical images, but it adds another dimension to our understanding of the God-world relation, and it both enlarges our idea of God and enables us to understand God as a single animating One who acts *in* all, and as the unifier *in whom* all act.

If the image of God as the soul of the world is not biblical (Psalm 103 cited by the rabbi, after all, does not actually envision God as a "soul."), let us track a bit of the history of some non-biblical usage. The best-known (to me!) ancient effort to construe the God-world relation in terms of a world soul and a world body is that of Plato's creation myth in the *Timaeus*. Plato tries to explain order in the world body in terms of the world-soul that encompasses the body and is the symbol of "the victory of reasonable persuasion over Necessity."[2] Some scholars are convinced that this is Plato's "ultimate God," a "world-soul ordering the world in light of the eternal idea."[3]

Later, some Stoics took up the idea that the universe is one and is pervaded by a *logos* or mind that they named the *Anima Mundi* (World Soul). As I say, not many Jews or Christians picked up on the idea, probably because they thought that it deprived God of transcendence. But one great Jewish thinker, Philo of Alexandria (ca. 20 BCE–54 CE), on at least one occasion asserted that "the soul of the universe is, according to our definition, God."[4] And I have been told that even St. Thomas Aquinas once said: "In his rule God stands in relation to the whole universe as the soul stands in relation to the body."[5] (Our parishioner John Lewis pointed out to me that both St. Bonaventure and Duns Scotus also likened the God-world relation to the soul-body relation. No doubt he learned this in EFM, but I was unaware of it). And then in the eighteenth century, the English poet, Alexander Pope (a professed Roman Catholic), said: "All are but parts of one stupendous whole, whose body Nature is, and God the soul."[6]

But it is only in recent times that persons have developed the image beyond the suggestion given in a one-liner. The important part has been in rethinking what a "soul" is. Too often in the past the soul was thought to be an unchanging spiritual substance that exists alongside, or even inside

2. Cornford, *Plato's Cosmology*, 160.
3. Hartshorne, *Insights and Oversights of Great Thinkers*, 37.
4. Hartshorne and Reese, *Philosophers Speak of God*, 77.
5. [See St. Thomas Aquinas, *ST* Supp. III, q. 80, a.1.]
6. Pope, *An Essay on Man: Epistle I*, line 267.

a body, but in such a way that the one (called by Descartes a *res cogitans*) has nothing to do with the other (called a *res extensa*); the soul could not interact with or be affected by the body. But, if we begin to think of the soul as the mind that decides, that acts in its body, via the brain cells and only then in the surrounding world, *but always first receives from* the world via the body and its brain information or data on which it can act, we can then understand the soul or mind as, not only acting in, but as receiving back, suffering, integrating, synthesizing, unifying, indeed changing, even as it is unified and gives orders back to the body by interacting with it.

The soul is, thus, "in" the body in the sense that each new instance of the soul acts *in* the immediately succeeding occasion of the brain, and so has effect in the rest of the body and, mediately, in the world beyond the body. But it is equally true, and no less important, to say that the body is "in" the soul, since the soul is the tightly knit series of occasions with the greatest capacity to receive and integrate into itself all the impulses of the prior occasions of the body as mediated through the brain. The soul is the *personal whole* that encompasses its body even as it *acts in* the body's constituent parts.

This way of thinking of the soul and its interactions with its body can take us some distance in developing the model of God as the universal soul that has the world of non-divine entities as its body. As with the human soul, the universal soul must be conceived as *temporal* and *social*. This is the basis for much talk of God as personal and acting personally. But whereas we tend to think of persons acting beyond themselves on those who are exterior to them, we need to remember that the primary way the soul acts is in its own brain cells, and thence in its body, and only by extension into the exterior world beyond it.

With God *there is nothing external*. God, the World Soul, acts immediately in his or her constituent parts. And they (we) act back in God in multiple ways; surely, we act in God by praying, but also by loving our neighbors as ourselves and, alas, by hurting, harming, trying to destroy our neighbors. Yet it is God in whom we live, and move, and have our being. It is God who gathers together and redeems all the broken parts.

> "Bless the Lord, O my soul, and all that is within me bless *her* holy name" (Ps 103:1; *alt.*)

10

THE EVOLUTION OF GOD

Advent 3—December 13, 2009
David R. Mason

Zephaniah 3:14-20

Philippians 4:4-9

Luke 3:7-18

O God, in whom we live and move and have our being: grant that, even as we know ourselves to have made a difference in the world around us, we also know that we make a difference to You who are our Ultimate Hope; and that when all peoples of the world are gathered into your granary, we will praise You who are our Redeemer. Amen.

I confess that I have asked for a specific Christmas gift this year. It is a book, naturally: *The Evolution of God* by Robert Wright. I admit to having skimmed, but not read carefully an earlier work, *Non-Zero: The Logic of Human Destiny*, in which Wright utilizes game-theory, "non-zero sum" game theory, to argue that "biological and cultural evolution move in a direction—toward broader and deeper complexity." And, although it is clear that Wright had long since abandoned belief in a "benign and omnipotent God," there are hints that a very thoughtful, intelligent person, deeply aware of the many things that can and do go wrong in this world—immense suffering, tragedy, evil empires, and dead-ends—sees, nevertheless, a "growth of goodness," the gradual overcoming of antipathy, and the possibility of a "cosmic architect" of a meaningful universe.

And now comes *The Evolution of God*. This is, indeed, hopeful in this the season of hope. Yet I also admit to having taken a peek at the table of contents (thanks to Amazon), and there I find what appears to be the story of the evolution or development of the "*idea* of God," rather than the idea of the "*evolution* of *God*," the idea of a God who, as the personal whole of reality, evolves toward ever deeper complexity as God interacts with an evolving, changing world.

In the table of contents I see chapter titles from "Primordial Faith" and "The Shaman" to "Polytheism" and "From Monolatry to Monotheism"; I see "Logos: the Divine Algorithm." I see chapters in the section called "The Invention of Christianity" from "What Did Jesus Do?" to "How Jesus Became Savior" and my heart skips a beat! What more hopeful sign could there be in this season of hope than to acknowledge Jesus as savior? And I see chapters on "The Triumph of Islam" and finally on "God Goes Global (Or Doesn't)."

Yet I do not sense here—and I may be wrong—the realization that the God for whom Jesus is the primal sacrament of freedom and love is, and must be, the God who *changes*, who *evolves* in ever greater complexity. The faith of some of the Hebrew prophets and our faith in Jesus as the Christ, implies and demands the clear recognition that the God for whom we all make a difference, the God of steadfast and ever-renewing love, is a God who changes, who evolves in complexity.

This was not understood clearly by early Christian thinkers, most especially theologians. Christian, Jewish, and Muslim theologians typically conceived God as static, as over-against the world, as able to act on the world, to manipulate events, persons, and things, but never to be acted upon, affected, changed by the world. The God of some of the Hebrew prophets who heard the cries of the people and was compassionate, the God and Father of Jesus who heard and responded to prayers, and who felt the pangs of the cross, and who said, "inasmuch as you have done it unto the least of these my brothers and sisters, you have done it unto me"—the God, therefore, who is affected, who changes, who is compassionate, was painted over by the image of a stern, unyielding God who cannot change and who will not be affected. The theologians had no idea of how God could be perfect unless God were *complete* and *unalterable*, and so they brushed aside the God of pure unbounded love—not unconditioned love, for love is by its very nature conditioned by those it loves—unbounded, inexhaustible love.

God is steadfast, to be sure, but not changeless or immutable. The fact *that* God exists is unalterable, but *God*—the actual individual being—is not immutable; the fact *that* God steadfastly loves and wills the best for God's creatures remains constant, but the God who loves is affected and changed by those loved. Moreover, even the content of God's will for good changes with the change of time and situation: "New occasions teach new duties, time makes ancient good uncouth."

This concept of a God who changes and evolves is largely the product of the modern world. It was, of course, implied by the biblical God, but it was not seen clearly until the sixteenth century, and not then by the Protestant Reformers, but by an Italian priest by the name of Socinus, who had to flee Italy to Poland because of heretical ideas, but who said that God was, in some ways, temporal with an open future. Socinus was followed in the nineteenth century by several minor figures and some major ones (Lequier, Schelling, Gustav Fechner, C. S. Peirce, William James, and others). But it was not until the twentieth century that Alfred North Whitehead and Charles Hartshorne, two philosophers, developed clearly and rigorously and fully the concept of God that is implied by the God represented by Jesus, the personal biblical God of love.

I do not sense an awareness of the modern idea that God actually, continuously evolves from the table of contents of Wright's new book. I may be wrong and I hope I am, because the idea is already well developed. It is a powerful tool for rendering our faith credible and, after all, faith should always be in search of understanding; it is also an antidote to the mad musings of fundamentalists.

I have frequently talked about this idea of God: "God as the World-Soul in whom we live and move and have our being"; "God as both absolute and relative"; God "who "makes things make themselves" ("The God of Waterbabies"). In fact, my dearest, most beloved critic says, "You always *only* want to preach about God!" I probably should plead guilty to that charge with the caveat that I occasionally mention the Browns and the Indians and even the Cavaliers, but they give us no reason to hope. And, in fact, I have raised the ire of some by preaching about politics, and there's little hope in that! But *God*: Ah yes, there is the ground and end of our hope.

God, I suspect, was the main focus of John's preaching even though he made a few references to sin and to doing good. God—the kingdom of God, the reign of God's pure unbounded love—was not only what Jesus proclaimed in his parables but what he incarnated in his life, his ministry, and his death and resurrection: God brought near.

This God, who enters into the deepest relationship with all creatures great and small evokes our response. And our response must be to love God's creatures and God with all our heart, soul, mind, and strength. This, essentially, is worship. But, if worship is to love God and God's creation, we see that we make a difference to God; we act in God's life in significant ways. Thus, God is not, as most of our forebears insisted, utterly immutable, but in fact changes, evolves. And, of course, God the supremely loving being is infinitely sensitive to all our needs. God is compassionate, God is affected, God changes.

We can appreciate the desire of our predecessors to insist upon God's constancy and the truth that God always is. But *God*, the actual being, who is the object of our faith and worship and who encompasses all reality, is shaped in part by what we do and think and feel. Therefore, God is temporal, relative, dependent, and changing; God evolves. God has a future as well as a past, and God actualizes new life from moment to moment.

This is good news. This is the ground and end of our hope. The ever-evolving personal whole of all reality in whom we live and move and have our being, touches our lives and is touched by our lives. This we now know through Jesus Christ our Lord.

11

REASON IN RELIGION

February 28, 2010
David R. Mason

Romans 12:1–2:

> I appeal to you brothers and sisters, by the mercies of God, to present your bodies as a living sacrifice, holy and acceptable to God, which is your reasonable worship. Do not be conformed to this world, but be transformed by the renewing of your minds, so that you may discern what is the will of God—what is good and acceptable and perfect.

O God, grant that my words and our hearts may be presented to You as a reasonable, holy, and living sacrifice; through Jesus Christ our Lord.

Recently I received a questionnaire from a high school student who was investigating the question whether or not religion is essential for a moral society. This question, I believe, is important for all of us to consider, and the student cast her net wide—at least I know that several of my colleagues received the questionnaire, and I suspect that she questioned a number of other adults, both religious and non-religious, in her community.

The questions I was asked to address were these:

1. Is reason or religion the center of morality?
2. Is religion to blame for most violence seen around the world?
3. Should religion stay completely separate from justice systems?
4. Is religion essential to maintain a moral society?

5. Is religion to thank for the teachings of good morals?
6. Is there a certain philosopher whose ideas of morality or a "god" you like or dislike?
7. Do you believe people raised with no religion are more likely to have worse morals than someone who is (raised with religion)?

You might think about how you would want to respond to various of these questions, but if you're like me you will be struck by the inherent ambiguity of all of the key terms—*religion, reason, morality, "god"*—so that you find it nearly impossible to give a straightforward "yes" or "no" to any of them. For instance, the last question, "Do you believe people raised with no religion are more likely to have worse morals than someone who is (raised with religion)?" itself raises many questions. What do you mean by "religion"? That's a word that covers a broad range of attitudes and behavior. What kind of a religion? Which religion? What do you mean by "morality" or "morals"? Explain please. What, in fact, is it to be "raised with no religion"? There are probably many different kinds of wholly secular attitudes and beliefs. Explain please. Be specific.

But it is the very first question that I want to bring before you: "Is reason or religion the center of morality?" Apart from the lack of clarity and precision attaching to words like "religion," "morality," and "reason," there is a hidden assumption here that skews the whole questionnaire, namely, that reason and religion are opposites, opponents in fact, and that religion is inherently irrational. The "or" in the question does not mean "one or the other or both." The center of morality, it suggests, must be *either* religion *or* reason, but *not both*; the two are wholly different. Religion, it assumes, is unreasonable; reason must be irreligious.

Let us challenge this assumption. It is one widely held by present-day secularistic or atheist critics of religion. It is also, let us be candid, held by many self-styled "Christian" opponents of modern secular thought. We must insist that these persons do not have an exclusive claim to the name "Christian." They are an odd recent deviation from normative Christianity. Call them "fundamentalists," although I am certain that they misconstrue the fundamentals of Christianity. And though they live daily with the fruits of modern scientific reasoning—they drive cars, they use computers, they brilliantly manipulate television—yet they want to insist that in matters of faith we must renounce reason, substitute bad religion for good science, and believe the most preposterous things: for instance, that the Bible presents

REASON IN RELIGION

a scientific account of the creation of the world and of humanity, and that biblical myths must be taken as historical facts. They seem to want to mimic the attitude of the third-century theologian, Tertullian, who contrasted human wisdom with the faith of the church: "What indeed has Athens to do with Jerusalem? What concord is there between the Academy and the Church?" and insisted about the death/resurrection of the Son of God: "It is credible *because* it's absurd. It is certain *because* it is impossible."[1] The fundamentalists think that to be faithful to God and to Jesus Christ, and so to be religious, they must shout down reason: scientific, logical, practical, and, frankly, religious reason.

Yes, there really is reason attached to, issuing from, and informing the deepest religious feelings, insights, and beliefs. I am thinking primarily of biblical religion, and I am taking "reason" to be any kind of critical thought that refuses to accept an answer because some "authority" (say, the Bible, or the church, or some noted modern thinker) said so, but thinks for itself and appeals to ordinary experience and to "logic."

Consider the Bible: the Psalms, while either in praise of God or in lament of bad fortune, often magnify reason. The prophets, while denouncing injustice and stupidity, appeal to our reason. The Wisdom literature actually deifies wisdom, suggesting that divine wisdom is the source and bedrock of human wisdom.

In the New Testament Jesus is encountered as a rabbi, a teacher. To be sure he often undermines conventional wisdom and the religious practices of the day, but he is never unreasonable in turning us to the kingdom of God. And, if his parables cut straight through our ordinary modes of reasoning about life, they cause us to think again, to rethink. John portrays Jesus as the incarnation of divine reason: "In the beginning was the Word [λογος; logos = 'word,' but also 'reason' or 'order'], and the Word was with God, and the Word was God. [The 'Word' of course, is also 'divine reason.'] . . . And the Word became flesh, and dwelt among us . . . full of grace and truth" (John 1:1, 14). Paul is the great champion of "faith." And let me be clear that faith is deeper than, and prior to, knowledge or reasoning. Paul knew this and even I am fully aware of it: first comes the mysterious experience of God's grace, and then the human response in faith, in trust, in confidence in God's love as making us right. But, because the humans who are thus justified by faith *are humans*, they must bring this to full consciousness and utilize their reasoning powers to the utmost, even if this

---

1. See Lane, *Harper's Concise Book of Christian Faith*, 19–20.

means rejecting previously held religious beliefs. So Anselm of Canterbury said: ours is "faith seeking understanding."[2] Reason does not precede faith, but it necessarily follows from it. So Paul, while insisting that we are "justified by faith apart from works of the Law," always tries to persuade us by appeals to reasons and to analogies. And in his greatest, most frankly reasonable, letter—that to the Romans—Paul appeals to the faithful to present themselves as "a living sacrifice, holy and acceptable to God which is your *reasonable* worship" (Rom 12:1). Several recent English versions (including the RSV and the NRSV) mistranslate *"logikein"* (λογικην) as "spiritual." But this is quite misleading. Paul frequently speaks of "the Spirit" and of "spiritual" and he always uses the word *"pneuma"* (πνευμα). But here he specifically uses the word based on *"logos," "logikein,"* in order to claim that worship must be reasonable or rational. Paul knew that to have faith and to live by the Spirit, and so to worship, was to be free and reasonable.

And so, in our very reasonable Anglican tradition we pray (in Rite One of the Holy Eucharist): "And here we offer unto thee, O Lord, our selves, our souls and bodies, to be a reasonable, holy, and living sacrifice" (Rite Two, while not saying this specifically, implies everywhere that worship is "reasonable;" e.g., "cleanse the thoughts of our hearts," several of the Prayers of the People, Eucharistic Prayer C, etc.). I realize, of course, that our worship is to be "holy and living," that is, spiritual and practical. But it is, too, reasonable. The entire Anglican tradition bends toward reason: it appeals to Scripture, which, as we have seen, is not unreasonable; it appeals to tradition, which for the most part (perhaps excepting Tertullian!) appeals to reason; it appeals to "the Spirit" and to "conscience" neither of which is opposed to reason even though both precede it; and it appeals to reason.

I could give examples from every century, but I appeal to only two: (1) the Cambridge Platonists of the seventeenth century who urged a "rational theology" in the teeth of the Puritans. The first of them, Benjamin Whichcote, set the tone for all the rest. Among his many "aphorisms" he said: "If you would be Religious, be Rational in your Religion" for "God speaks to us inwardly, by the *Reason of our* minds: not against Reason, or without it." And, "Nothing spoils human nature more than False *Zeal.*" "The *Good Nature* of an Heathen is more God-like than the furious zeal of a Christian." Also, "True Religion hath done only good in the world; *Superstition* (which is the Counterfeit of Religion) hath done the worst and greatest Mischiefs."[3]

---

2. Anselm, *St. Anselm*, 2.
3. Whichcote, *Moral and Religious Aphorisms*, nos. 339, 384, 274, 114, 928, 929.

(2) The Broad Church movement of the nineteenth century, in particular Charles Kingsley. You have heard me on Kingsley's "Water Babies" and the idea of a God who "makes us make ourselves." It was Kingsley, I was reminded in a review of the movie *Darwin*, who wrote to Darwin on the publication of *The Origin of the Species*, that this was wholly compatible with the deepest springs of Christian religion. Yes, to be sure, there were bishops who were shocked, but Kingsley and all advanced Anglicans saw this work as a triumph of science *and* of religion. So you have heard me say that I learned of Darwin and of the theory of evolution positively in Sunday School (this was not, by the way, in the nineteenth century!). But, alas, when I went to high school it was a biology teacher who told me that "evolution" was "the work of the devil."

Naturally, a young student could hardly stand up to his teacher. But whenever you hear an atheist deride all religion as irrational superstition bring that person up short; "in quietness and in confidence" explain the many ways that reason is woven into the warp and weft of our religion. And whenever you hear a fundamentalist or a biblical literalist attack the theory of evolution or promote creationism or intelligent design, somewhat more passionately and with feeling explain that this is *not* Christian, and show the person why: it is contrary to reason.

Ours is a *reasonable*, holy, and living worship of the One God, especially as decisively revealed through Jesus Christ.

Amen.

12

MORAL IMAGINATION

Sixth Sunday of Easter, May 9, 2010
St. Paul's Episcopal Church
David R. Mason

John 14:23–29

May the words of my mouth and the meditation of our hearts be pleasing unto Thee, O Lord our God, who art the Savior and Redeemer of all the peoples of the earth.

I begin with a string of passages from Scripture, or Scriptures, and then, in the manner of David Brooks, from what I've been reading recently. If these passages do not, initially, seem to have much in common or to connect the dots, I hope that I may unpack them in such a way as to eke out some moral imagination that makes for tolerance and goodwill among the peoples of the earth, particularly the peoples of the "Abrahamic religions"—Judaism, Christianity, and Islam.

1. From today's gospel passage (John 14:25–26): "I have said these things to you while I am still with you. But the Advocate, the Holy Spirit, whom the Father will send in my name, will teach you everything and remind you of all that I have said to you."

2. From the Holy Qur'an (Surah 61:6): "And remember, Jesus the son of Mary, said O Children of Israel, I am the messenger of Allah sent to you, confirming the Law which came before me, and giving Glad Tidings of a Messenger to come after me, whose name shall be Ahmad (i.e., Mohammad)."

MORAL IMAGINATION

The third and fourth are taken from the King James translation of the Bible:

3. Isaiah 7:14 (KJV): "Behold, a virgin shall conceive, and bear a son, and shall call his name Immanuel."

4. Matthew 1:21–23: "And she shall bring forth a son, and thou shall call his name, Jesus, for he shall save his people from their sins. Now this was done, that it might be fulfilled which was spoken of the Lord by the prophet, saying, 'Behold a virgin shall conceive and shall bring forth a son, and they shall call his name Emmanuel, which being interpreted is, God with us.'"

5. Finally, a piece from the penultimate chapter of Robert Wright's *The Evolution of God*, which chapter is called, "The Moral Imagination":

> The moral imagination like other parts of the human mind, is designated to steer us through the successful playing of games—to realize the gains of non-zero-sum games [i.e., those in which both sides prosper or win] when those gains are to be had . . . The moral imagination is one of the main drivers of [religion as seen in this book]; the tendency to find tolerance in one's religion when the people in question are people you can do business with . . . *Our understanding of the motivations of others tends to come with a prepackaged moral judgment.* Either we understand their motivation internally, even intimately, relate to them, extend moral imagination to them, and judge their grievances leniently—or we understand their motivations externally and in terms that imply the illegitimacy of their grievances . . . The bulk of westerners and the bulk of Muslims are in a deeply non-zero-sum relationship, yet by and large aren't very good at extending moral imagination to one another.[1]

Now, let me return to the first two passages to begin my journey: I confess that I rarely paid attention to the passage in John: "The Advocate, the Holy Spirit, whom the Father will send in my name, will teach you everything." There are other, more significant, sayings in chapter 14—"I am the way and the truth and the life . . ." "Whoever has seen me has seen the Father," "Those who love me will keep my word and my Father will love them," and "Peace I leave with you, my peace I give unto you." BUT . . . "the Advocate, the Holy Spirit"?! This seems like an odd bit of John's theology. Yet there are four places when John has Jesus speak of the Holy Spirit as the

---

1. Wright, *The Evolution of God*, 420–21.

"Advocate" or "Counselor" (14:15; 14:26; 15:26; 16:7), evidently indicating some sort of divine legal aid for the disciples. And I learned in seminary that the word used is "Paraclete" (παρακλητος), but this did next to nothing for me *until* I came upon the Muslim interpretation of the passage from the Qur'an that I read; "Remember Jesus . . . said . . . I am the messenger of Allah sent to you . . . and giving Glad Tidings of a Messenger to come after me whose name shall be Ahmad."

It seems that the Muslims believe that "Ahmad" is a translation of the Greek word, "*paracletos*" (Paraclete). Therefore, it is obvious to the Qur'an that Jesus had foretold the coming of Mohammad by name, as an Advocate, or helper and teacher!

Perhaps you will understand my initial amusement, but then irritation at hearing this repeated. The practice of blatantly mistranslating and misunderstanding another's Scripture in order to make it point ahead to, and foretell, one's own hero as Prophet or Messenger is dodgy business; it is playing fast and loose with history and with fact. And to clothe it with irrefutable divine authority—"This is scripture whereof there is no doubt" (Surah 2:2)—is to make far greater mischief. It is to exclude the "other" from any claim to finality or truth by asserting authoritatively, "We have it, and you don't." It is the beginning of a zero-sum argument: my gain is your loss.

But wait! Haven't we seen this sort of thing before? Indeed, we have. And that is why I selected numbers 3 and 4 with this in mind:

#3: (Isa 7:14): "Behold, a *virgin* shall conceive, and bear a son, and shall call his name Immanuel."

#4: (Matt 1:21–23): "She shall bring forth a son . . . Jesus . . . that it might be fulfilled [as] spoken by the prophet . . . 'Behold a *virgin shall be with child and shall bring forth a son, and they shall call his name Emmanuel.*'"

To be sure, all of us now know (I hope!) that the Isaiah passage, which purportedly spoke of a "virgin," is a *mis*translation of a straightforward statement by Isaiah either about the young king's wife or about someone else: "Look, the *young woman* is with child and will bear a son." The passage was *not* the prediction of something odd that was to happen seven hundred years hence. But because the Greek Septuagint translation of the Hebrew Bible used the word "virgin," here the Christian writer of the Gospel latched onto it in order to lock in a so-called "prophecy" by Isaiah of a virginal conception and a son, Jesus, called Emmanuel. This, too, was *playing fast and loose with history and with fact*.

MORAL IMAGINATION

You and I can understand the mistake, and will be inclined to grant some leeway to Matthew for his misguided effort to establish the virgin birth on the basis of a made up "prediction" by Isaiah. We are naturally prone to accept and to deal gently with the peccadilloes of our own group. But put yourselves in the shoes of a Jewish reader of Matthew, and I guarantee you that you will experience the same irritation that I felt with the Muslim claim that Jesus predicted the coming of Mohammad!

So what are we to do? Snipe at one another? Find faults with the others' religions (Jewish, Christian, Muslim—depending on where you are sniping from)? Or, find fault with *all* religions ("Religion poisons everything," says Christopher Hitchens)? Neither of these options is illuminating nor is it helpful to humankind, but both are championed by extremist minorities in a particular religion or in the secular world (the secular extremists are those who think that to love this world entails hating all religion).

Nor are these "true" to the best in religions or to the trajectory that religion has followed through the ages from tribal religions to world religions with a universal God who cares for and redeems all people. Muslims, Jews, and Christians, at least, are all true monotheists whose God, at best, loves all creatures. We must seek to identify the best in the "other" and we must search for the best in their religion. To be sure, as we stretch to understand the others we will find reasons to disagree, but perhaps we will expose our own faults and stupidities and so try to rectify these in interrelationship with the others. This is what interreligious dialogue always tries to do. If we employ a "moral imagination," as the greatest religionists have done, we will activate the tendency to be tolerant of the others even as they differ bitterly with us. As Wright suggests, even in deeply troubled times such as the present, we may "understand their motivations internally, even intimately, relate to them, extend moral imagination to them and judge their grievances leniently."

I have been concerned today primarily with Muslims, Jews, and Christians. But I should extend the reach of moral imagination to include *all* religions and, in fact, irreligion or atheism. Moreover, I might well be concerned about the divisions within the Christian household—divisions between Catholics and Protestants, liberal and conservative Christians. In every case, whenever we encounter any "other," if we try to understand *their* motivations internally we may endeavor to relate to them, and so extend moral imagination to them, and judge their grievances leniently. Only this way will we "know the truth, and the truth will make [us] free." (John 8:32)

Moral imagination requires deep faith and courage. But if we continually try to exercise it we can produce non-zero-sum, or win-win results and God's world will be a better place. If we do not the extremists (e.g., Osama bin Laden, Anwar al-Awlaki, or Franklin Graham) will win, and chaos will ensue. I know we are better than that.

I offer these reflections and these examples in the name of God in whom all of us "live and move and have our being" and on behalf of all religions and all charitable reason everywhere. *Amen.*

LECTURES AND ESSAYS

That many meanings of "God" are intellectually untenable does not prove that all conceptions of a supreme reality worthy of worship must be so.

CHARLES HARTSHORNE,
REALITY AS SOCIAL PROCESS

God is not to be treated as an exception to all metaphysical principles, invoked to save their collapse. He is their chief exemplification.

ALFRED NORTH WHITEHEAD,
PROCESS AND REALITY

When the Western World accepted Christianity, Caesar conquered; and the received text of Western theology was edited by his lawyers. . . . The brief Galilean vision of humility flickered throughout the ages uncertainly. In the official formulation of the religion it has assumed the trivial form of the mere attribution to the Jews that they cherished a misconception about their Messiah. But the deeper idolatry, of the fashioning of God in the image of the Egyptian, Persian, and Roman imperial rulers, was retained.

The Church gave unto God the attributes which belonged exclusively to Caesar.

In the great formative period of theistic philosophy . . . three strains of thought emerge which, amid many variations in detail, respectively fashion God in the image of an imperial ruler, God in the image of a personification of moral energy, God in the image of an ultimate metaphysical principle. . . . The three schools of thought can be associated respectively with the divine Caesars, the Hebrew prophets, and Aristotle. . . .

There is, however, in the Galilean origin of Christianity yet another suggestion which does not fit very well with any of the three main strands of thought. It does not emphasize the ruling Caesar, or the ruthless moralist, or the unmoved mover. It dwells upon the tender elements in the world, which slowly and in quietness operate by love; and it finds its purpose in the present immediacy of a kingdom not of this world. Love neither rules, nor is it unmoved; also it is a little oblivious as to morals. It does not look to the future; for it finds its own reward in the immediate present.

God's role is not the combat of productive force with productive force, of destructive force with destructive force; it lies in the patient operation of the overpowering rationality of his conceptual harmonization. He does not create the world, he saves it: or more accurately, he is the poet of the world, with tender patience leading it by his vision of truth, beauty, and goodness.

What is done in the world is transformed into a reality in heaven, and the reality in heaven passes back into the world. By reason of this reciprocal relation, the love in the world passes into the love in heaven, and floods back into the world. In this sense, God is the great companion—the fellow-sufferer who understands.

ALFRED NORTH WHITEHEAD,
"GOD AND THE WORLD," IN *PROCESS AND REALITY*.

1

THE NEW ATHEISM

St. Paul's Church
May 4, 2008

(This and the two following talks were prompted by two parishioners, Tom Nobbe and Bill Welsh, who at different times and in different ways urged me to address the challenge of the "New Atheism." I wish to thank and acknowledge them.)

Several years ago I was handed a copy of Sam Harris's book, *The End of Faith*, with the question: "How should we respond to this?" A year later a member of the adult forum pressed me to respond to the new atheists, and so I do. I confess that I had not heard of Sam Harris when I got his first book, but I had studied and come to terms with the reasoning of some of the most thoughtful and challenging skeptics and atheists from the eighteenth century to the present: David Hume in the eighteenth; Feuerbach and Marx in the nineteenth; Freud, Sartre, Camus, J. N. Findlay, and Antony Flew in the twentieth. I thought that rational atheism had reached a dead end.[1] I knew that Antony Flew, perhaps the most formidable atheist of the last half century had recently made an about-face to come to a belief in Aristotle's "unmoved mover," an "immutable, immaterial, omnipotent, and omniscient Being."[2] More significantly for me, the brilliant French existentialist Albert Camus, in his last published article prior to his death in 1960, famously rejected what was taken to be his own previous philosophy of "the absurd" or what comes to "ultimate despair." He said, "no one can believe in a literature of despair . . . The absurd can be considered only as a

---

1. See Alister McGrath, *The Twilight of Atheism*.
2. Flew, *There is a God*, 155.

point of departure ... In any case how can one limit oneself to the idea that nothing has sense and that we must despair of everything? Without going to the bottom of the matter, one can at least observe that, in the same way that there is no absolute materialism, since merely in order to fashion this word it is already necessary to say that there is something more in the world than matter, there is no total nihilism. From the moment that one says that all is nonsense, one expresses something that has sense ... A literature of despair is a contradiction in terms."[3] Camus realized that "sheer materialism" and "total nihilism" are the legitimate parents of atheism, and so was saying that there *is* a ground of meaning and worth in the universe after all.

Nevertheless, I was clearly wrong to have assumed that atheism was on its last legs. In fact, had I been attentive I would have noticed a rise and growth of vocal atheism correlative with an equally rapid growth of fundamentalism and irrational religion, a religion that makes claims that fly in the face of science and common sense. There may not be a causal relation between the two—fundamentalism and atheism—but they have grown together and bid fair to crowd out reasonable religion with its love of both God and human reason.

In any case after Harris's first book a batch of scathing attacks on religion as a "pernicious and outdated superstition," which "poisons everything," and upon the "God Hypothesis" as sheer "delusion" came tumbling forth. Richard Dawkins's *The God Delusion*, Daniel Dennett's *Breaking the Spell: Religion as a Natural Phenomenon*, Christopher Hitchens's *God is Not Great: How Religion Poisons Everything*, Harris's second work, *Letter to a Christian Nation*, and Victor Stenger's *God, The Failed Hypothesis: How Science Shows God Does Not Exist* appeared in quick succession, and seem to have captured the attention of the literate (if not always well-informed) public.

Today I wish to examine what I take to be the major argument—or *the assumption* and *the claim*—that lies at the heart of this type of atheism, and then to consider several of their other "refutations" of belief in God. Next Sunday I will bring forth several arguments for the reasonableness of belief in God, and a reasonable way of making sense of the "personal" God of the monotheistic traditions. On the third Sunday I will examine the attack upon religion as "pernicious ... superstition."

The leitmotif running through and under all the works of the new atheists is that "God" or any divine entity is a "fiction" or a "delusion" or a "superstition" that *science*—i.e., *natural* science utilizing the *empirical*

---

3. Camus, "The Riddle," 85.

method—can and does show to be false. According to these thinkers, the hypothesized "God" turns out, on the basis of empirical investigation, to be, not a fact, but a fiction.

This is most clearly articulated in Dawkins, but I believe it is fairly close to the surface in the others (they typically assert that "reason" refutes the God Hypothesis, but reason most often turns out to confined to the work of natural sciences). For instance, Dawkins says "the God Hypothesis" is that "there exists a superhuman, supernatural intelligence who deliberately designed and created the universe and everything in it, including us."[4] Now, admittedly, he uses the word, "supernatural" here, but it is not meant seriously, because he supposes the belief to be about a very superior being of the same sort as we are, a natural being writ large, so to speak. Hence, God's work and very being are subject to empirical falsification or verification. Hence Dawkins asserts that "the presence or absence of a creative super-intelligence is unequivocally a *scientific* question,"[5] and "God's existence or non-existence is a scientific fact about the universe, discoverable in principle, if not in practice."[6]

Sam Harris is not too far from this when he insists that believers "should be obliged to present evidence for [God's] existence—and indeed for his benevolence"[7], and "the success of science often comes at the expense of religious dogma . . . Every religion makes specific claims about the way the world is . . . Such claims are intrinsically in conflict with the claims of science, because they are claims made on terrible evidence."[8]

Christopher Hitchens, despite his state of high dudgeon about religion, applies mostly *reason*, and not science, to the object of religion. Even so, when he criticizes William Paley's "Argument from Design," which he takes to be the best that theology has to offer, he appeals to the science since Darwin (many theologians had preceded him in seeing that Darwin had provided a much more adequate ground of adaptation). And he shows his hand when he says, "I was educated by Sir Karl Popper to believe that a theory that is unfalsifiable is to that extent a weak one."[9] Had he really been educated by Popper he would have understood Popper's point to be that a

---

4. Dawkins, *The God Delusion*, 31.
5. Dawkins, *The God Delusion*, 58–59; my italics.
6. Ibid., 50.
7. Harris, *Letter to a Christian Nation*, 51–52.
8. Ibid., 63–64.
9. Hitchens, *God is Not Great*, 81.

theory that is unfalsifiable is not a *scientific* hypothesis; Popper was aware that there are principles of metaphysical reasoning that do not appeal to natural scientific evidence.

Even Dennett, who is a philosopher and remarks that he is neither a biologist nor a theologian, wants to "set about studying religion scientifically."[10] Admittedly, "religion" is not "God," but Dennett seems to think that, insofar as religion is shown to be a "natural phenomenon," the *object* of religion, God, is thus shown by science to be nothing but a human construct.

"How Science Shows God Does Not Exist" is the subtitle of Victor Stenger's book *God: The Failed Hypothesis*.[11] This subtitle, "How Science Shows God Does Not Exist," fairly straightforwardly sums up the assumption and the main argument of all of our present-day atheists. Since they "know" (i.e., assume) that "reality" is constituted solely by the physical universe, that which the natural sciences can investigate, and that science shows that God does not exist, it is, for them, an open-and-shut case: "reality" is finite and is what can be investigated by empirical research or known by natural scientific reasoning; examination of the phenomena of the natural world discloses nothing non-natural and science can, moreover, give natural explanations for what had been claimed to be the work of God; hence, there is no God. With this conclusion safely tucked away their "refutations" of various "arguments" or "proofs" for God become merely a matter of dismissing these arguments as specious or outmoded reasoning: If you know something is wrong and you're fairly clever, it is easy enough to dismiss arguments without carefully considering what they have had to say.

Let us examine their assumption and their claims. It is, of course, very difficult to establish clearly that our authors assume that "reality" is constituted solely by the physical universe or that which the natural sciences can investigate, because they never say this clearly, but their constant appeal to science strongly suggests it. If it is true, however, that they assume that reality is exhausted by what science can investigate, they are "begging the question." That is, they *assume the truth of what is in dispute or what is to be proved*: "no God" is built into the assumption that all reality is finite and can be known empirically. By assuming that the natural world exhausts all of reality they have already concluded that there is nothing more than the natural, physical universe—nothing "supernatural," nothing divine,

10. Dennett, *Breaking the Spell*, 20.
11. Stenger, *God, The Failed Hypothesis*.

nothing "spiritual" (beyond patently human emotions that can be investigated empirically), nothing "transcendent," nothing "mysterious" (other than a problem that can be solved), NO "God." *QED*. But this, you see, is not a rational argument; it is begging the question, and it should be exposed for what it is.

Let me now examine the claim, and then respond. Dawkins puts it as clearly and forthrightly as anyone: "God's existence or non-existence is a scientific fact about the universe, discoverable in principle, if not in practice ... The presence or absence of a creative super-intelligence is unequivocally a scientific question."[12]

The claim is that "God" must be an object among others discoverable by scientific methods or shown to be non-existent or extinct by science. But for centuries reasonable believers have understood that, whatever the word "God" stands for, the reality behind the word (whatever it is that we worship) is *not* one thing among others; it is, rather, the ground and end of all finite things. When believers say that God is the greatest conceivable reality, or the One alone worthy of worship, they mean that "God" is a reality whose mode of existence is radically unlike that of creatures who can be perceived by the five senses and tested by scientific experiment. God is a reality whose *nonexistence is logically impossible*, i.e., one who cannot fail to exist no matter what occurs in the world. This is a claim that must be assessed by *reason* (or philosophy) and it is the implication of *faith*. (Be very careful here; "faith" is not, as some think, "belief without evidence" or, as Sam Harris says, "nothing more than the permission religious people give one another to believe things strongly without evidence."[13] Rather, faith is the "ineradicable confidence in the final worth of our existence,"[14] that all humans exist with, and faith, in a religious sense, is always "seeking understanding."[15]) At any rate, whatever "God" might be, God is never to be thought of as a finite entity to be examined, verified or falsified by the scientific method. So, sophisticated inquirers have understood that the "God question" is *not* a scientific one, but a religious or a philosophic one.

Even the less sophisticated believers of earlier times who plainly spoke of God in anthropomorphic terms (God as father, king, mighty warrior,

---

12. Dawkins, *The God Delusion*, 50, 58–59.

13. Harris, "Afterword to the Vintage Books Edition," *Letter to A Christian Nation*, 110.

14. Ogden, *The Reality of God*, 37.

15. Anselm, *St. Anselm*, 2.

one who walks in the garden, etc.) always sensed that God was "spirit" whose existence was "from everlasting to everlasting" (Ps 90:2). In other words they understood that God was not a natural entity. And however much their myths seemed to intrude God and divine activity into the world that science can and must investigate, they always tried to hedge: "For my thoughts are not your thoughts nor are your ways my ways, says the Lord. For as the heavens are higher than the earth, so are my ways higher than your ways, and my thought than your thoughts" (Isa 55:8–9).

The awareness that God and divine ways are the concern not of science but of religion and that religion is a legitimate way of knowing, has, of course, been recognized by many scientists in our day. For instance, Peter Medawar, a Nobel Prize-winning scientist (who emphasizes that "science is incomparably the most successful enterprise human beings have ever engaged upon") observes that there are "questions that science cannot answer, and that no conceivable advance of science would empower it to answer . . . Questions [such] as: How did everything begin? What are we all here for? What is the point of living?"[16] And Stephen Jay Gould insisted that what he called the two "magisteria of science and religion" were non-overlapping: "The magisterium of science covers the empirical realm: what is the universe made of (fact) and why does it work this way (theory). The magisterium of religion extends over the questions of ultimate meaning and moral value."[17] Dawkins fumes over this: "I simply do not believe that Gould could possibly have meant much of what he wrote," he says. And he asks, "Does Gould really want to cede to *religion* the right to tell us what is good and what is bad? The fact that it has nothing *else* to contribute to human wisdom is no reason to hand over to religion free license to tell us what to do."[18] I don't need to comment other than to remark that when one refuses to get the point it is a common tactic to say that one's opponent didn't really mean what he said, and then to fulminate that religion has contributed nothing to human wisdom.

A similar charge is brought by Sam Harris (who also denounced Gould as a "quisling") against the National Academy of Science. That group issued a statement: "At the root of the apparent conflict between some religions and evolution is a misunderstanding of the critical difference between religious and scientific ways of knowing. Religions and science answer

---

16. Peter B. Medawar as cited in McGrath, *The Dawkins Delusion?*, 38–39.
17. Cited in Dawkins, *The God Delusion*, 55.
18. Ibid., 57.

different questions about the world. Whether there is a purpose to the universe or a purpose for human existence are not questions for science. Religious and scientific ways of knowing have played, and will continue to play, significant roles in human history . . . Science is a way of knowing about the natural world. It is limited to explaining the natural world through natural causes. Science can say nothing about the supernatural. Whether God exists or not is a question about which science is neutral."[19] Far from seeing the profound point of this Harris denounces it for "its lack of candor," because, as he says, "scientists live in perpetual fear of losing public funds, so the NAS may have merely been expressing raw terror of the taxpaying mob."[20] Again: miss the point and impugn the integrity of the scientists. I will say to Harris's credit (and to Dawkins's, too) that he is rightly angry over the habit of some religions to intrude religious claims into the work of the natural world and to give theological explanations for natural processes ("creationism" and "intelligent design" are notable instances). But that is no excuse for attempting to establish a totalitarianism of science whereby all truth, beauty, and goodness are arbitrated and determined by science or its camp-followers. The more thoughtful scientists do not want it, and it is unreasonable, dehumanizing, and an attempt to stifle the Spirit.

With their "Sword against the Spirit" firmly in hand, Dawkins, Hitchens, and Harris attend to several of the so-called arguments for God in order to dismiss them, and bring forth one powerful argument against belief in God. Here are four that I will examine: (1) Aquinas's "five ways" and (2) the ontological argument (both treated by Dawkins); (3) the argument from design (considered by most, but best treated by Hitchens); and (4) the problem of evil (brought forth as decisive by Harris).

Dawkins's cavalier treatment of Aquinas's "five proofs" for the existence of God, and the whole edifice of Aquinas's very complex doctrine of God, is whisked away in three pages. He dismisses the first three arguments all of which rely on "the idea of regress and invoke God to terminate it. They make the entirely unwarranted assumption," he says, "that God himself is immune to the regress."[21] Dawkins fails to see that God, here, is the prime mover, like the ground of all being, and not understood as the first of a series. Moreover, the *idea* of God—not the "unwarranted assumption"—is of a being without beginning and without end, infinite in being,

---

19. Cited in Harris, *Letter to a Christian Nation*, 62–63.
20. Ibid., 63.
21. Dawkins, *The God Delusion*, 77.

for whom terminating the regress simply does not apply. Dawkins might have attacked the assumption that Aquinas holds with Aristotle, that God, as prime mover, is "moved by no other," in any sense, but he doesn't. He mentions dubious properties of God such as "omniscience, omnipotence" and others, but does not make the effort to understand the arguments, the ideas, or the vast amount of intelligent discussion that Aquinas has engendered. This is because he *knows* all the while that Aquinas's arguments are "perniciously misleading."[22] This is not a refutation, but a curt dismissal.

Dawkins's treatment of the ontological argument, although six pages in length, is less well informed. He quotes Anselm's *first form* of the ontological argument, but utterly fails to see that Anselm's real argument is its *second form*, which works with the understanding that God is a being whose *nonexistence is logically impossible*, a being that "cannot be conceived not to exist." Dawkins simply does not mention anything that Anselm said in the second form of his argument. Yet he calls on Bertrand Russell, who himself failed to get Anselm's point, and Kant who, likewise, missed the heart of Anselm's reasoning (the second form). Oddly, he quotes Norman Malcolm (who is one of the twentieth-century philosophers who *did* see that there are two forms of the ontological argument), but he quotes Malcolm articulating Kant's point about *the first form* of Anselm's argument: "The doctrine that existence is a perfection is remarkably queer. It makes sense and is true to say that my future house will be a better one if it is insulated than if it is not insulated; but what could it mean to say that it will be a better house if it exists than if it does not exist?"[23] It is evident that Dawkins did not read Malcolm or understand him. Malcolm argued in his now famous article that Anselm has two different pieces of reasoning, and he showed that the heart of Anselm's reasoning was to be found in the "second ontological proof," which maintains that "a being whose *nonexistence is logically impossible* is 'greater' than a being whose *nonexistence is logically possible*." And Malcolm says: "Previously, I rejected *existence* as a perfection. Anselm is maintaining in the remarks last quoted [the second form] not that existence is a perfection, but that *the logical impossibility of nonexistence is a perfection*. In other words *necessary existence* is a perfection. His first ontological proof uses the principle that a thing is greater if it exists than if it does not exist. The second proof employs the different principle that a thing is greater if it necessarily exists than if it does not

---

22. Ibid., 78.
23. Norman Malcolm as cited in ibid., 83.

necessarily exist."[24] That Dawkins simply does not understand the argument is indicated by his report that he had used the "ontological argument" to prove that pigs can fly—and he says that theologians and philosophers "felt the need to resort to Modal Logic to prove that I was wrong."[25] Yes, that is the point: the *mode* of existence of God ("necessary existence") is quite other than the *mode* of existence of all others (finite beings who can be examined by science!), which is "contingent existence" (the kind that might or might not have existed).

I'm sorry to smother you with what must appear to be arcane nit-picking, but you need to know that there has been serious philosophical discussion of the ontological argument in the twentieth century that Dawkins wantonly ignores. (I hope to make this clearer next Sunday in my talk, "Faith in God is Not Unreasonable," and in a piece I've written called "Three Recent Treatments of the Ontological Argument.")

Christopher Hitchens's attack upon one form of the argument from design is fairly good, if not very temperate. He begins by dispatching William Paley's argument from the "discovery" of a watch in the fields to the certainty of a watchmaker. Essentially he echoes Lord Macaulay's observation that "Paley had put his creaking, leaking cart in front of his wheezing and broken-down old horse. Fish do not have fins because they need them for the water, any more than birds are equipped with wings so that they can meet the dictionary definition of an 'avian.' . . . It is exactly the other way about: a process of adaptation and selection."[26] Darwin and Darwinians got it right, that by natural selection among random mutations (or "blind chance") the long process evolved. And, as Michael Shermer put it, "Evolution also posits that *modern organisms should show a variety of structures from simple to complex, reflecting an evolutionary history rather than an instantaneous creation.*"[27]

Hitchens proceeds through a long, rambling series of musings designed, it seems, to show both his having read lots of scientists and scientific reports and his own brilliant writing style. He clearly indicates that the consensus is that creation is ongoing, random, and frequently not well designed; hence, he adds, that the creation is without the need of a "stupid

---

24. Malcolm, "Anselm's Ontological Arguments," reprinted in Plantinga, ed., *The Ontological Argument*, 141, 142.

25. Dawkins, *The God Delusion*, 84.

26. Hitchens, *God is Not Great*, 78–79.

27. Cited in ibid., 81.

notion of intelligent design."[28] He notes, as have others, that approximately 98 percent of all the species that have ever appeared have lapsed into extinction and that most organisms are poorly designed, and so asks: "Why *do* people keep saying 'God is in the details'? He isn't in ours," Hitchens snaps, "unless his yokel creationist fans wish to take credit for his clumsiness, failure, and incompetence."[29]

I see no reason to argue with this particular rejection of these particular arguments from design. I think that one could make a philosophical case that the *whole universe* is more or less orderly, given that there is also plenty of chance and randomness, and then suggest that there needs to be an orderer (because chance limited only by chance is chaos). But this must wait.

The last of the atheists' arguments against God that I want to take up is what is known as "the problem of evil." It has been raised and addressed by many thoughtful and sensitive people since the time of *Job*, and it should not be taken lightly. Sam Harris puts the matter with candor and effectiveness:

> Somewhere in the world a man has abducted a little girl. Soon he will rape, torture, and kill her. If an atrocity of this kind is not occurring at precisely this moment, it will happen in a few hours, or days at most. Such is the confidence we can draw from the statistical laws that govern the lives of six billion human beings. The same statistics also suggest that this girl's parents believe—as you believe—that an all-powerful and all-loving God is watching over them and their family. Are they right to believe this? Is it good that they believe this?
>
> No.
>
> The entirety of atheism is contained in this response.[30]

Harris, of course, gives many specific examples of destruction and death, suffering and loss (Katrina, where, as he says, "poor people died talking to an imaginary friend," Shiite pilgrims trampled to death while reciting the Qur'an, the Holocaust, the Rwandan genocide, etc.). His point is that all of this casts doubt upon a benevolent, omniscient, and omnipotent God, and that an atheist is bound to call into question God's power and/

---

28. Hitchens, *God is Not Great*, 85.
29. Hitchens, *God is Not Great*, 85.
30. Harris, *Letter to a Christian Nation*, 50–51.

or goodness or, more likely, conclude that God does not exist: "Of course," he says, "people of all faiths regularly assure one another that God is not responsible for human suffering, but how else can we understand the claim that God is both omniscient and omnipotent? This is the age-old problem of theodicy, of course, and we should consider it solved. If God exists, either He can do nothing to stop the most egregious calamities, or He does not care to. God, therefore, is either impotent or evil . . . There is another possibility, of course, and it is both the most reasonable and least odious: the biblical God is a fiction . . . whom most sane people now ignore."[31]

How do we respond? I do not think we can let God off the hook by saying that God gave us free will and that it is because of our sinful free choices that evil and suffering entered the world. In the first place there is massive suffering and death that result from natural causes; bad things happen that are not the result of human free decisions. Secondly, to speak of "God giving us free will" assumes that God is in total control, the puppet-master who pulls all the strings. And, the critic will ask why God could not have created a world in which free choices were always for the good or why God would not intervene if things are about to go wrong. Moreover, if God knows the outcome of events ahead of time, which is the way that "omniscience" is usually understood, there really is no free choice and so God is responsible for the bad things that occur. Moreover, if God has total power to manipulate all things and the power to run roughshod over all natural causes and does not constantly use that power for the good, God is negligent or wicked. We must rethink our ideas of "freedom," "omniscience," and especially of "omnipotence" if we are to deal with the problem of evil.

First, "freedom." Having some form of freedom is, I believe, intrinsic to any actual entity in any world at all. Humans, of course, and probably other higher vertebrates, have freedom of choice that is inevitably limited by causal conditions. And at every level of being "all the way down," so to speak, we find a degree of randomness, chanciness, open possibilities, and spontaneity that are the foundation of freedom. Yet nothing is *wholly determined* either by past causes or by God. We do not have to assert that "God *gave* us freedom." Causality and freedom are both part and parcel of any world at all. So we can search for *how* God works with the natural causes *and* the inherent freedom that jointly produce a partially orderly, partly disorderly, partly creative world.

---

31. Ibid., 57.

So, what about "omniscience"? Since the sixteenth century increasing numbers of persons who have thought seriously about divine knowledge have concluded that it makes no sense to think that God could know "from all eternity" or ahead of time the outcome of everything. As Socinus said in the sixteenth century, "God must know the real as that which it is, the past as past, the present as present, the future as future . . . The future, however, consists of what only possibly *may* occur," not of what actually has occurred.[32] In other words the future consists only of possibilities, not of actualities. "Future events"—events that have not yet happened—are *not there* to be known. Therefore, not even God could know as actual what is merely a possibility. Hartshorne put it succinctly: "*God does not already or eternally know what we do tomorrow for, until we decide, there are no such entities as our tomorrow's decisions.*"[33]

We do not need to abandon omniscience as characteristic of genuine divine knowledge. We need to divest it of absurdities. We can say that God knows in detail all that has occurred in the past and all that is presently occurring. And we can assert that God knows the full range of possibilities that lies ahead of us, but never, ahead of time or from eternity, precisely which of those is to be actualized. Keep constantly in mind the inherent freedom and the ever-new possibilities that are fundamental constituents of our world.

Finally, there is "omnipotence"—literally, "*all* power." The literal meaning suggests that God has a monopoly on power. But that cannot be so, because to be anything at all is to be a center of power or to have power. So, given that there are any finite entities at all, God could not be omnipotent in that sense. Nor, as St. Thomas Aquinas knew, does omnipotence imply that God can do what is logically impossible to do. So, for instance, to determine the outcome of anything—if things have any freedom—is logically impossible and so not a part of God's power. Still, religious people, *and their atheist critics*, have regarded divine power under the rubric of coercion, manipulation, unilateral power, and the power to determine the outcome of events. But this answers as little to genuine religious needs as to the demands of logic. It has been remarked that the power to determine things and to eliminate all problems is actually what sinful people would like to be able to do were they God. Or we could say it is a very childish view of what adult power is like: "I often wish I were a King, and then I

32. Socinus in Hartshorne and Reese, *Philosophers Speak of God*, 226.
33. Hartshorne, *Omnipotence and Other Theological Mistakes*, 39.

could do anything . . . If I were only king of Greece, I'd push things off the mantelpiece . . . If I were king of anything, I'd tell the soldiers, I'm the king."[34] But, in fact, the power to move about tin soldiers is in the hands of very small children. And the power to mold clay into pots is in the hands of average adults. Yet, as has been said, "[t]he power required to lead adult human beings (and not tin soldiers) is incomparably greater precisely because those who are led retain power of their own. To think of God as more like the potter or the child is to degrade his power. The power that counts is the power to influence the exercise of power by others"[35]

So, how must we understand "the power to influence the exercise of power by others" without attempting to manipulate or coerce them or determine what they do? I think we can regard this power as "persuasion": the persuasion of *reason* or, alternatively, the power of "being with" another, even suffering with the other in his or her suffering without being diminished. This is the power of *love*. I know that will sound hokey, and just what you would expect from a religious person, but think about it: the power of love (however we construe this) is greater than the power to manipulate or to kill. And, if the supreme being is the one who is supreme by virtue of being present to *all*, is affected by all and in turn influences (somehow) all, is interactive with all beings, great and small, can suffer with those who suffer, and thereby can redeem them, the problem of evil or the problem of suffering is addressed. The God whose love "moves the sun and the other stars"[36] *is* the God whose deepest reality is revealed on the cross as suffering love: "The great companion—the fellow-sufferer who understands,"[37] I think this is the best way to address the "problem of evil."

---

34. Milne, "If I Were King," in *The World of Christopher Robin*, 111
35. Cobb, *God and the World*, 89.
36. Dante, *Paradiso*, 303.
37. Whitehead, *Process and Reality*, 351.

2

FAITH IN GOD IS NOT UNREASONABLE

May 11, 2008

Happy Mother's Day. Happy Day of Pentecost. If I seem to be "speaking in tongues" do not either credit or blame the Holy Spirit! Ideas about God and the language in which these ideas get framed have traveled far since the early days, and there is no reason to think that language and thought about whatever is ultimate should be any less demanding or difficult for ordinary educated persons to grasp than language about physics or neuroscience. Philosophy and theology require concentrated thought, the ability to make distinctions, and an openness to new ways of thinking. And, frankly, during the modern period, when natural science has made so many tremendous strides and has produced so much wonderful knowledge about our world, philosophy and theology have also developed several new ideas about ultimate reality and have produced new ways of thinking about it. Unfortunately, these have gone largely unnoticed.

Last week I talked about why the so-called new atheism is wrong and has largely misfired in its attack upon belief in God. The gravamen of my rebuttal was that the new atheists *assume* that "reality" is constituted wholly, and without remainder, by the physical universe, the finite world that can be empirically examined by natural science. And they conclude from this that natural science measures *all* truth. For the new atheists, therefore, anything that is not natural, anything that cannot be measured by science, "deity" for example, has been eliminated from the outset. This is not reasoning or rational argumentation; it is an unexamined *assumption*. And it is one that is reinforced with the *claim* that "science shows that God does not exist." But is the assumption justified? And can *science*

FAITH IN GOD IS NOT UNREASONABLE

show that God does not exist? Whatever we might mean by "God" we can never mean that God is one being among others in this realm that science examines, an empirically falsifiable or verifiable entity. Had they grasped this simple point, they would never have rejected so angrily Stephen Jay Gould's point that "the magisterium of science covers the empirical realm: what the universe is made of (fact) and why does it work this way (theory). The magisterium of religion extends over the questions of ultimate meaning and moral value"; or the statement of the National Academy of Science: "Religions and science answer different questions about the world . . . Science is a way of knowing about the natural world. It is limited to explaining the natural world through natural causes. Science can say nothing about the supernatural. Whether God exists or not is a question about which science is neutral."

After making this point I was able to look at several of their ways of mistreating Aquinas's "five ways" and Anselm's "ontological argument" for the existence of God. Then I examined the very real difficulty with the particular pre-Darwinian version of the so-called "argument from design" as well as the "problem of evil" so powerfully set forth by Sam Harris. The latter problem, however, could not possibly show that God does not exist, only that certain ideas of God are a "fiction." But in attending seriously to this issue we are required to rethink what "supreme power" really means, whether God knows all future as already determined, and the inevitability of freedom and open possibilities in any "world" whatsoever. Rethinking the meaning of *omnipotence, omniscience,* and *freedom* casts a new light on the problem of evil.

Having seen that the arguments of the new atheists are by no means conclusive or persuasive we should turn about and try to show that *faith in God is not unreasonable.* I put it this way because, while I believe that no "proof" one way or another will ever be wholly persuasive, to dismiss all reasoning about God as a matter of "rationalization" in the Freudian sense is to cut short all reasonable discussion. As has been well said: "Between 'convincing to all' and 'convincing only to those already committed to the conclusion' there is ample room for intermediate possibilities."[1]

It is with the hope of unpacking some of the "intermediate possibilities" that I now turn our attention to several pieces of reasoning that may help to make sense of the nearly universal belief that there is a "more" to existence, that there *is* something that "stands beyond, behind, and within

---

1. Hartshorne, *Creative Synthesis and Philosophic Method,* 275.

the passing flux of immediate things; something which is real, and yet waiting to be realized . . . something that gives meaning to all that passes, and yet eludes all apprehension; something whose possession is the final good, and yet is beyond all reach . . . the ultimate ideal and the hopeless quest."[2]

The first piece of reasoning that I want you to consider seriously is the so-called "ontological argument for the existence of God" made famous by St. Anselm of Canterbury. And I beg you to put aside what you may have learned in a first philosophy course: that the argument is specious and has been rejected by all fair-minded persons. In fact, it has rarely been examined in its fullness. The argument is complex; in fact, there are *two distinct forms* of Anselm's argument—really, two distinct arguments. This was rarely seen until recently. The best known, and most frequently attacked argument, is the one that is found in chapter 2 of Anselm's work, *Proslogion*. The more subtle argument, typically neglected because it was taken as the conclusion to the argument of chapter 2 rather than as a distinct line of reasoning, is that which comes out in the third and fourth chapters of the *Proslogion* and in Anselm's reply to the monk, Gaunilo. It will help us to see the difference if we first lay out the argument of chapter 2 and look at some criticisms before turning to the radically different piece of reasoning that is in the third and fourth chapters of *Proslogion* and in Anselm's Reply to Gaunilo. I set forth the argument of chapter 2 in seven steps:[3]

1. Anselm begins with a definition: God is "a being than which nothing greater can be conceived."

2. Even the "fool" who says "in his heart that there is no God" understands this definition when he hears the word: therefore the object can be said to exist "in the understanding."

3. A distinction is made between existing "in the understanding" and existing "in reality."

4. Existence in reality is greater than existence (merely) in the understanding.

5. But "that than which nothing greater can be conceived" exists in the understanding

    (see # 2).

---

2. Whitehead, *Science and the Modern World*, 267–68.
3. See Anselm, *St. Anselm*, 7–8.

FAITH IN GOD IS NOT UNREASONABLE

6. And yet, if "that than which nothing greater can be conceived" existed *only* in the understanding, it would *not* be "that than which nothing greater can be conceived"

> (see # 4). Or, as Anselm puts it, "If that, than which nothing greater can be conceived, exists in the understanding alone, the very being, than which nothing greater can be conceived, is one than which a greater can be conceived." But this is an impossibility.

7. Therefore, the being than which nothing greater can be conceived must exist both in the understanding and in reality.

This argument turns on the distinction between "existing in the understanding" and "existing in reality," and it has elicited much negative response. Very shortly after *Proslogion* appeared, a monk, Gaunilo, made a reply "In Behalf of the Fool," saying that one could easily understand the idea of a "lost island" that is more excellent than all lands. But to insist, as if by a logical inference, that such an island, which is held in the understanding, must therefore exist in reality, is preposterous, he said, the very height of folly.[4]

The best known refutation of this sort came at the hands of the philosopher Kant, who said that "existence" is "not a real predicate," which is to say that however many ways we may describe a thing we do not give it better definition if we say, "and it exists": "By whatever and however many predicates we may think a thing—even if we completely determine it—we do not make the least addition to the thing when we further declare that this thing *is*."[5] Norman Malcolm, as we saw last week, put Kant's point this way: "The doctrine that existence is a perfection is remarkably queer. It makes sense and is true to say that my future house will be a better one if it is insulated than if it is not insulated, but what could it mean to say that it will be a better house if it exists than if it does not?"[6] The argument is false because it is senseless.

It mattered little that Anselm's argument applied *only* to "the greatest conceivable being," and not to ordinary things, as Anselm had said in reply to Gaunilo. The point had been made, and was universally accepted, that

---

4. Anselm, *St. Anselm*, 150–51.
5. Kant, *Critique of Pure Reason*, 505.
6. Malcolm, "Anselm's Ontological Arguments," in Plantinga, ed., *The Ontological Argument*, 139.

the supposed distinction between "existence in the understanding" and "existence in reality" was a false distinction; when we hold something in the understanding we conceive it *as existing*. Therefore, it will not do to argue that a thing is greater if it exists in reality than if it is only conceived in the understanding, because to conceive it *is* to conceive it *as existing*.

So let us grant that Anselm's first argument is faulty or specious. This criticism, however, does not touch the nerve of the reasoning that is central to Anselm's *second argument*, which is to be found in chapters 3 and 4 of *Proslogion* and in Anselm's full response to Gaunilo. In order to see this as a totally different piece of reasoning it will be helpful to quote portions of this argument highlighting certain words and phrases:

> It (the being "than which nothing greater can be conceived") assuredly exists so truly that *it cannot be conceived not to exist*. For it is possible to conceive of a being which cannot be conceived not to exist; and this is *greater* than one which *can be conceived not to exist*. Hence, if that, than which nothing greater can be conceived, can be conceived not to exist, it is *not* that, than which nothing greater can be conceived. But this is an irreconcilable contradiction. There is, then, so truly a being than which nothing greater can be conceived to exist, that it cannot even be conceived not to exist; and this being thou art, O Lord, our God. So truly, therefore, dost thou exist, O Lord, my God, that *thou canst not be conceived not to exist* . . . To thee *alone*, therefore, it belongs to exist more truly than all other beings, and hence in a higher degree than all others . . . No one who understands what God is can conceive that God does not exist . . . For God is that than which a greater cannot be conceived. And he who thoroughly understands this, assuredly understands that this being so truly exists that not even in concept can it be non-existent . . . That than which a greater cannot be conceived, if it exists, cannot be conceived not to exist. . . . Of God alone it can be said that it is impossible to conceive of his nonexistence.[7]

Note that this line of reasoning is totally different than the argument of chapter 2. Here Anselm says that that greatest conceivable being, God, has a peculiar or unique *type* or *mode of existence*: "God *cannot be conceived not to exist*." All the rest of us are such that we *can* be conceived not to exist. Moreover, a being "which cannot be conceived not to exist" is greater than

---

7. Anselm, *St. Anselm*, 8–9, 10, 156, 161. These are from chapters 3 and 4 of *Proslogion* and from Anselm's "Reply to Gaunilo."

one "which *can* be conceived not to exist." So, we would never say of a being that can be conceived not to exist that it is that than which nothing greater can be conceived. If we genuinely conceive the greatest conceivable being we are conceiving one that cannot be conceived not to exist. As Anselm says in chapter 4, "No one who understands what God is can conceive that God does not exist . . . For God is that than which a greater cannot be conceived. And he who thoroughly understands this, assuredly understands that this being so truly exists that not even in concept can it be non-existent." Again, in his Reply to Gaunilo, Anselm says: "That than which a greater cannot be conceived, if it exists, cannot be conceived not to exist." And, "Of God alone it can be said that it is impossible to conceive of his nonexistence."

Now, the major point that Anselm is making here is, *not* that "existence is a predicate," (which Kant decisively refuted) but that *the logical impossibility of non-existence is a predicate*." It is the defining predicate of the unique being, God.

To put the argument in more modern terms, we see that Anselm argues that a being said to have "necessary existence" (that is, it cannot not exist or it cannot fail to exist in some state or other) is greater than one that has merely "contingent existence" (that is, it can be conceived not to exist, or it might never have existed, or it might cease existing, etc.). Hence, the greatest conceivable being must be one that has necessary existence or one whose nonexistence is logically impossible. And, if we conceive God correctly, we conceive God as necessarily existing; and, if God necessarily exists, God exists! Even, when, in his Reply to Gaunilo (see above), Anselm seems to qualify his argument by saying, "if it exists," I do not think he is making the senseless assertion: "If God exists, *but he might not*, God exists necessarily." For this would be tantamount to asserting that God has both necessary *and* contingent existence; and this is an impossibility. What I think Anselm means is that, "if the idea of God makes sense, that is, if we conceive God correctly, we see that the idea entails that God exists necessarily.

But this brings up a different matter about which we need to be candid. Anselm seems to have thought the only options were "necessary" (nonexistence is logically impossible) and "contingent" (nonexistence is logically possible) types of existence and, because God cannot be contingent, God must be necessary. Yet today we can see that there are three categories or types of "existence" that we must consider. The third type is "impossible existence." This would be one *that cannot be conceived to exist* or one whose existence is logically impossible, e.g., a "round square."

So the three categories of existence are:

A. Necessary existence: that which cannot be conceived not to exist, or that whose nonexistence is logically impossible, or that which must exist somehow no matter what occurs.

B. Contingent existence: that which might not have existed, or that which does not exist, but might exist, or that which might cease existing (all ordinary beings).

C. Impossible existence: that which cannot be conceived to exist, or that whose existence is logically impossible (e.g., a round square, a married bachelor, or a being who is *in all respects* necessary, but in some respects contingent).

Anselm has effectively shown that "contingent existence," and all the arguments and modes of verification associated with it, is utterly inapplicable to the greatest conceivable being, God. But rather than leaving us with but one alternative—"God necessarily exists"—Anselm has really left us with two: either "God necessarily exists" or "God is impossible." If the idea of "necessary existence" can be shown to make sense (as in the claim, "'something exists' is necessary") and, in particular, if the idea of the necessary existence of a particular being is not nonsensical or contains no contradictions, then we can assert with some confidence that God necessarily exists. But, if the idea of "necessary existence" could be shown to be senseless or, if claims about the necessary existence of God contain contradictions, then God's existence is impossible or God could not possibly exist.

The idea of "necessary existence," I believe, cannot be shown to be senseless; but if claims about God *as necessary* contain contradictions, then, as J. N. Findlay saw, the claims "entail [God's] necessary non-existence."[8] That is, if we assert, as much of the theological tradition (and its modern critics) have done, that God must be *wholly* necessary (merely "eternal," unmoved, changeless, non-relational, without possibilities, without a future, etc.) and yet knows, loves, interacts with contingent, temporal beings, then *this* "God" (and only this one) is an impossibility like a "round square."

The way to avoid this dilemma is to make another important distinction that the philosopher, Charles Hartshorne, has made: that between the bare "existence" of any individual and its "states of existence" or its

---

8. Findlay, "Can God's Existence Be Disproved?," in Plantinga, ed., *The Ontological Argument*, 120.

FAITH IN GOD IS NOT UNREASONABLE

"actuality." We all know how to make this distinction with respect to ordinary individuals: from start to finish, an individual person, we say, has the same existence. The existence or genetic identity of that individual never varies; John Smith is always Smith, no matter what. Yet, the actual state of the individual, his or her "actuality," changes from moment to moment; "Smith *now*" is not the same as "Smith *then*"; the content, the *state* of existence, the *actuality* changes. "New occasions teach new duties; time makes ancient good uncouth."[9] So, when we meet a friend after years we exclaim, "My, how you've changed." The underlying "you," the individuality or bare existence has not changed, but the "particular you" is different; the actuality, "Smith now" is changed from "Smith then." Actuality, or the particular state of existence, changes.

This distinction must be applied in spades to God. The bare existence of God is necessary; it cannot be other than it always is; God cannot fail to exist no matter what occurs. But "God," the actual being, changes continuously. The state of existence, "God now," is changed from the prior state of existence, "God then," by virtue of interacting with all finite, contingent, temporal beings. God can and must exist necessarily. God can and must interact with, know, love, evaluate, redeem all ordinary, temporal beings, and that everlastingly; God does and must change. There is no contradiction in asserting both that "God's *existence* is *necessary*" and that "God's *states* of existence are *contingent*." Therefore, we can have a God who *exists necessarily*, but in different *states of existence* that are contingent upon the interactions with ordinary beings; we can have a God whose existence is necessary and immutable, but whose states of existence change.

Now let us consider two additional pieces of reasoning that lead us into the vast middle region where it may be said that belief in God is not unreasonable. First, let us begin with *faith* properly understood. I recognize that when we begin with "faith," many will say, "But we all know that faith is irrational or, at least non-rational; faith is opposed to reason or is, at best, unreasoning." But is this really the case? What is faith, after all? Surely, it is *not* a matter of "believing what you know ain't true" or an attachment to something that emotionally satisfied us as children and would keep us in a state of childish dependence even still, although I realize it appears in this guise frequently. I believe that the basic faith of humanity is something given to every human as it exists, something that is prior to any particular "religious faith": it is the conviction that everything we do or experience makes a difference in the

---

9. Lowell, "Once to Every Man and Nation," *The Hymnal: 1940*, # 519.

world about us. To be or to do anything is to be *something that matters*. We can say that this is a basic confidence that existence is meaningful or worthwhile, because as we do anything at all and as we experience anything at all, we realize, however dimly, that we do make a difference in the world. We are something that matters: *to ourselves, to others, and inevitably to the whole of which we and others are parts.* Another way to say this is that to be anything at all, no matter how small or seemingly insignificant, is to be a *value* for our ongoing selves, for others, and for the whole. To speak of "values" is not to say that all acts or experiences are positive values; some are negative or evil. But all acts make a difference in the world, good or bad. Nothing can annul this, because once we have done anything it cannot be undone; it is registered for evermore in reality, in the encompassing whole of which we are all parts. Thus, the whole of reality for which everything makes a difference is the ground of our ineradicable confidence that we are some thing that matters.[10] Is this "whole of reality" merely the indifferent expanding universe? Is it *nirvana*? Is it, perhaps, God?

Theism is the conviction that the abiding, but ever-expanding whole is the *personal whole of reality*; it is the One "in whom we live and move and have our being" (Acts: 17:28), the One "unto whom all hearts are open, all desires known, and from whom no secrets are hid."[11] Thus, we are parts that make a difference to the whole. I do not think it is too much of a leap to suppose that the encompassing reality for which we make a difference is *personal*, because every time we sense that our actions, our lives, are worthwhile, we almost inevitably think that they are worthwhile *for someone.*

Faith is the inescapable trust that we make an abiding difference. But where? In the encompassing whole of reality. What is this, but the personal whole, the One who knows, loves, and redeems our every action—God?

If the reasoning from the basic faith of humanity leads to the idea of God as the recipient and recorder of all our acts, the One who synthesizes all achieved value, *the redeemer*, the next line of reasoning suggests that there must be One of cosmic scope who gives order to what otherwise would be mere chaos. This is, of course, the intuition that lies at the base of the creation story in the first chapter of Genesis.

In the modern world we have even more reason to bend in this direction. For we are intensely aware of the dynamic, radically temporal character of all reality. Ours is a world rife with open possibilities, shot through

---

10. See Whitehead, "Civilized Universe," Lecture Six, in *Modes of Thought*, 143–71.
11. *The Book of Common Prayer*, 323.

and through with chance. When we take seriously the dynamic, open character of the world and reflect deeply upon it, it seems that nothing actual would ever come about were there not an interactive being of cosmic scope to bring the infinite sea of possibilities within manageable limits. That is to say, given any situation riddled with infinite possibilities and the risk of destruction that incompatible past actions entail, no world would ever emerge apart from the operations of a universally present orderer. Chance limited only by more chance is mere chaos. But there is, in fact, a world with some order—not a rigid, all-determining order, to be sure, but an order nonetheless to the dynamic, changing world. Without a being able to synthesize all that occurs in the world and to envision the ideal possibilities in their relevance to each actual situation, there could be nothing more than chaos. An ordering entity seems to be a necessary element in the situation presented by the actual world: God the orderer or creator.

Of course, we must understand that, if God is the *supreme agent* in shaping the world at any moment, God is *never the sole agent*. The assumption that God was the sole agent of creation was the mistake that classical philosophers and theologians made. It gives rise to the strict notion of omnipotence that makes the problem of evil such a problem: if God *determined* the outcome of everything why is there evil in the world? Why, in fact, speak of "open possibilities" at all? But, of course, the world we live in is one where all creatures make a difference and so are partial causes of what comes to be. It is, also, a world where there is always chance and new possibilities. It is a world of conflict. Yet, it is *a world* and *not* mere *chaos* or sheer nothingness. And this requires a being of universal scope to be present to all, and to synthesize all immediately past acts that might have been in conflict, and to present to each new emerging occasion an aim ideal to its actual situation. But the occasion actualizes itself. Without God there would be nothing but chaos, that is, nothing actual. God is, thus, the orderer, the supreme creator with whom we are co-creators. And so God is both the ground of order and of novelty.

I recognize that the foregoing "arguments" or pieces of reasoning about God are by no means conclusive. But taken together, and together with the widespread conviction that there *is* something "beyond, behind, and within the passing flux of immediate things" that is ultimate, they help to show that faith in God is not unreasonable. More specifically, in fact, they have argued that it is reasonable to think that God exists necessarily, but in continuously contingent states; that God knows, loves, and interacts with all beings; that

God not only continuously creates, but everlastingly redeems the creatures that constitute the world. God is the personal whole of which we are all parts, the One in whom we live and move and have our being.

3

REMARKS ON THE ATHEISTS' ATTACK ON RELIGION

May 18, 2008

If we attend closely to the works of the new atheists we see immediately that they are concerned not only to deny God but to impugn religion. What they see—and perhaps the *only* thing they see—is religion on its dark side: religion as evil, the very source of hatred and the engine of violence in the world; religion as a weaver of fantasies, fictions, fairy tales, and lies that hold people in ignorance, that psychologically repress or enslave people keeping them in childish obedience, oppressed and unwilling to grow into maturity ("Dare to know" is what Kant said was the dictum of the Enlightenment). In the words of Marx, religion is "the *opium* of the people"; it keeps us in chains that bind us to an "illusory sun."[1] And, like Marx, the new atheists are proclaiming "reason" as that which will break the chains and reclaim us from our opium addiction. If we see only what they see there is much to commend their attack.

Christopher Hitchens says "religion poisons everything," and he gives examples of the deleterious effects of religions. He cites the tawdry claims of miracles, the "grotesque history of religion and sex," the many, many instances of religion promoting killing, from biblical times to the present, the patent lies that religionists have indulged in to maintain power over people's minds—and more.

---

1. Marx, "Toward the Critique of Hegel's Philosophy of the Right," in *Basic Writings on Politics and Philosophy,* 263.

Sam Harris links religion and terror, pointing specifically to Muslim jihadists, but not neglecting Jewish, Christian, and Tamil terrorists, killers, etc. He is especially repulsed by religious literature, in particular the Bible and the Qur'an as fantasy that, he believes, contain next to no facts, and no wisdom whatsoever, and that, in an enlightened scientific age, should be ignored or cast aside, "forgotten as a dream dies at the opening day."[2]

There is too much truth in many of the charges that they bring forth for those of us who love religion, and *our* religion in particular, to neglect the charges. The main fault I find with them is that they too readily, and without any sense of nuance, generalize from "some to *all*"; they tar all religion with the brush of fanaticism, violence, and stupidity. It has long since been recognized by religious people themselves that the many negativities are what the seventeenth-century Cambridge Platonist Benjamin Whichcote identified as "the Counterfeit" of "True Religion." Specifically, in this respect, Whichcote said: "Nothing spoils human Nature more that false zeal. The Good nature of an Heathen is more God-like than the furious Zeal of a Christian . . . *True* Religion hath done only good in the world; but Superstition which is the *Counterfeit* of Religion, hath done the worst and the greatest Mischiefs"[3] . And by "counterfeit" as "superstition" Whichcote meant that unyielding, narrow-minded conviction that I alone possess the truth, and that my way is the exclusive path to God. He was aiming his barbs at the extremes of his day: Puritans and high churchmen. Unfortunately, the counterfeits of true religion are very much with us today, and they often claim themselves to be the "one, true, religion." If the atheists unmask them, that is all to the good.

To be sure, the cocksure critics of religion highlight the obvious examples of stupidity and viciousness in religious literature and life. And, in doing so, they ignore the many counter-instances of genuine wisdom, integrity, and care for the poor and the wretched of the earth, love for all beings including those who are alien to us, all of which are grounded in the love for God that is also found in religious life and literature. But it will not be my job to catalogue a list of counter-examples and so to engage in a kind of tit-for-tat with the new atheists.

Rather, I would like to address two issues that routinely come up: (1) the Bible as the inerrant "Word of God" particularly when the *words* of

---

2. Isaac Watts, *The Hymnal 1982: according to the use of The Episcopal Church* (New York: The Church Hymnal Corporation, 1985), # 680.

3. Whichcote, *Moral and Religious Aphorisms*, # 274, 114, 928–29.

REMARKS ON THE ATHEISTS' ATTACK ON RELIGION

Scripture turn out to be childish, stupid, far-fetched, evil, repressive, etc.; (2) closely allied with this is the well-publicized efforts of the biblical fundamentalists to have "Creationism" and "Intelligent Design" taught in science classes as a *scientific* alternative to evolution.

1. About the Bible. From the days when the various biblical texts were written it has been realized that they *were written by humans*, in many different contexts, and at different times. They may have claimed to have been "inspired" by God, but that could only hold fast in some cases. No one would claim, for example, that Ps 137:9, "Happy shall they be who take your little ones and dash them against the rock," or the many injunctions to kill people for minor offenses in Leviticus, or the claim by the author of 2 Thessalonians that the returning "Lord Jesus revealed from heaven with his mighty angels" would "inflict vengeance on those who do not know God," are inspired by God. They are inspired by the worst of superstitions. When biblical authors say, "thus spake the Lord," or we proclaim, "the Word of God," they/we know full well that these are the partial insights and claims of deeply religious people in particular situations, and NOT the Words of God. Close readers of scriptural texts, from the earliest days, have realized that we simply cannot take the laws, the claims, and the words of Scripture literally as words of God. But they were convinced that the Scriptures contained much that was significant, that was holy. Therefore, they looked for figurative, and sometimes allegorical, ways of interpreting the texts, lately seeing much as profound mythology. All this is epitomized by Reinhold Niebuhr: "It is important to take Biblical symbols seriously but not literally."[4]

For the past two hundred years biblical scholars have employed critical-historical methods to investigate the many layers of the Bible (incidentally, the critical-historical investigation of church history and of the Bible were some of the best early modern uses of the historical method). Many people realize that the Bible contains many different types of language: e.g., myth, legend, poetry, wisdom sayings, prophecy, legal and ritual codes, ethics, history, letters to churches, proclamations of good news, and stories with meanings that point to God as "pure unbounded love," among others. Biblical critics know the difference between "myths" and "legends." Myths are "stories of the gods" or of divine interaction with the world and so about the ultimate meaning of our existence—they must inevitably be "demythologized" or interpreted existentially. Legends are fanciful stories about the "heroes" of our tradition. Neither myths nor legends should be taken at face

---

4. Niebuhr, *The Nature and Desting of Man, Vol. II*, 50.

value as objective history. And the "history" in the Bible is heavily larded with "spin" and often blended with legend. It should be said that it is the devoted biblical researchers themselves who have spotted the legend and spin. And "prophecy" is typically not so much fortune telling or predicting future events as it is criticism of the political, social, and religious status quo in the name of the Lord; it is, as is often said, "speaking truth to power." The heart of biblical religion, I believe, is: "Hear, O Israel, the Lord our God, the Lord is One; you shall love the Lord your God with all your heart, with all your soul, with all your mind, and with all your strength; and you shall love your neighbor as yourself." This is, of course, a combination of Deut 6:5 and Lev 19:18 pulled together by Jesus (see Mark 12:29–31). Clearly, Jesus did not originate the sayings, but it was the genius of Jesus, I believe, to see that they are inextricably joined together, and as Matthew has Jesus saying, "On these two commandments hang *all* the law and the prophets." (Matt 22:40. Jesus, perhaps, *ought* to have cited Lev 19:35, "You shall love the *alien* as yourself," but he didn't.) Even so, the parable of the Good Samaritan (Luke 10:29–37) identifies a "neighbor" as anyone, even an alien within the land, who shows mercy, thus making the point that biblical religion insists that we must love God with the totality of our being and everyone whom God loves, including those who are alien to us, as ourselves.

The biblical religious view is (in the words of a philosopher, and not a biblical scholar) "that God is the one conscious life which includes all lives, without prejudice to their freedom and distinctions"[5] The philosopher who said this presses the matter further: "Each of us," he says, "is but a fragment of reality . . . Religion is what, for good or ill, we do with this fragmentariness . . . We cannot fully achieve true worship until we humbly accept our fragmentary status . . . In sober truth, a human individual is but a fragment, neither the whole nor the lord of the whole . . . Those who do not worship must in some way be forgetting or denying their real situation"[6] The biblical stories and heroes rarely forget or deny our fragmentary status; nevertheless, they inevitably sense that we are "something that matters" to God in whom "we live and move and have our being."

2. Now, about fundamentalism and evolution. Let me simply point out that it is not *Christians* who oppose evolution, but a *particular brand* of modern Christianity grounded in "fundamentalism," that has tried to usurp the name "Christian." Consider the two most high profile recent cases.

---

5. Hartshorne, *Wisdom as Moderation*, 83.
6. Ibid., 84–85.

REMARKS ON THE ATHEISTS' ATTACK ON RELIGION

In the Arkansas case of 1981 (Rev. Bill Mclean et al., plaintiffs vs. The Arkansas Board of Education et al., defendants), which brought the Arkansas Board of Education, and the Governor and the Assembly, to trial for having mandated the teaching of "Creationism" as science. The individual plaintiffs were largely Protestants and Roman Catholic bishops together with individual Christian clergy and parents. With the exception of one biology teacher, the plaintiffs were not scientists. They were supported by various Jewish groups.[7] The plaintiffs, of course, got legal help from the ACLU, and they brought in scientists as witnesses, but they also brought in high profile Christian theologians as witnesses (Langdon Gilkey being one of them). What I want you to see here is that it was largely mainline (mostly Christian) religionists that brought the case to trial, who championed evolution, and who opposed fundamentalism.

Much the same can be seen in the highly-publicized Dover, PA "Intelligent Design" case (Tammy Kitzmiller et al. v. Dover Area School District et al.). Once again the plaintiffs were largely mainline Christians, one a biology teacher. And one of the key scientific "witnesses" for evolutionary science, in opposition to "Intelligent Design" as science, was Kenneth Miller, a cell biologist and Professor of Biology at Brown University *and* a professed Roman Catholic (among other things he has written *Finding Darwin's God*). Moreover, a key theological witness for the plaintiffs was the Roman Catholic theologian John Haught who has written *God after Darwin: A Theology of Evolution*.

All of the religious plaintiffs in these cases were comfortable with the realization that the Bible is neither a scientific treatise nor a strict historical record of the world from the crack of dawn to the crack of doom. They understood full well that the Genesis account of creation is not to be treated as a scientific account, but is rather a mythological story of our ultimate origin. Thus, they knew that to take the biblical symbols literally, as both fundamentalists and their adversaries, the new atheists, do is to miss the point badly; it turns a powerful *religious message* into a piece of bad science. More than that, it treats the divine as something this-worldly, finite. Hear what the theologian, Paul Tillich, said about biblical literalists, or fundamentalists:[8]

> The character of the symbol to point beyond itself to something else is disregarded. Creation is regarded as a magic act which

---

7. Gilkey, *Creationism on Trial*, 269.
8. Tillich, *Dynamics of Faith*, 51–52.

happened once upon a time. The fall of Adam is localized on a special geographical point and attributed to a human individual. The virgin birth of the Messiah is understood in biological terms, resurrection and ascension as physical events, the second coming of Christ as a telluric, or cosmic, catastrophe. The presupposition of such literalism is that God is a being, acting in time and space, dwelling in a special place, affecting the course of events and being affected by them like any other being in the universe. *Literalism deprives God of his ultimacy and, religiously speaking, of his majesty.* It draws him down to the level of that which is not ultimate, the finite and conditional . . . *Faith, if it takes its symbols literally, becomes idolatrous.*

I believe that the biblical fundamentalists who promote creationism or intelligent design *as science* are not only counterfeiters, but idolaters. Let me add what I said in a sermon on the Second Sunday of Easter on the resurrection account in John, namely, that I think the new atheists and the fundamentalists are *twins*, a little like Tweedledum and Tweedledee, who would "fight until six, and then have dinner" but "hit everything within reach . . . whether [they] can see it or not."[9] Here is the relevant part of that sermon:

> You will, no doubt, not be surprised that I recur most often to the story of "Doubting Thomas": what is right and what is wrong with him; what is sound, healthy, and spiritually fruitful in Thomas's attitude and approach, but what is radically wrong and misguided about his naïve, but very modern, assumption that all truth is to be gotten by sense perception, is that all reality is physical or material reality.
>
> What is right, sound, healthy, and helpful? I think that we need to see that the persistent, questing skepticism that Thomas represents is not the antithesis of faith, but close to its very heart. Of course, in all search for truth we must ask questions and not too readily accept easy answers. But this is even more so, and more unlimited, when we are searching for the ground of the ultimate meaning of our existence, as Thomas was. Thomas had sensed deity and salvation, the ground of authentic existence for him, in his master and teacher, Jesus. But hope for a meaningful existence seemed to have been dashed with the death of Jesus. Yet he learned that Christ was alive in the midst of his companions, and so he risked the uncertainty; he reached out in passion for the

---

9. Carroll, *The Annotated Alice; Alice's Adventures in Wonderland and Through the Looking Glass*, 243.

infinite. To be sure, Thomas refused to accept what we might call "hearsay evidence," the word of others. He needed to experience Christ alive, God-for-us, for himself. So he returned. He did not give up in despair; he did not reject the quest for ultimate meaning by attending only to the quotidian round, the humdrum eking out of a living, or even by amassing great wealth. Thomas returned to find Christ alive, and he exclaimed: "My Lord and my God!" His doubt was a questing doubt, a risk-taking doubt. It was a faith or trust in the intangible, the unseen and unfathomable depth of love represented by the risen Jesus.

And we can admire and emulate Thomas here. The apostle of doubt is the apostle of faith, and insofar as we appropriate that questing, doubting faith, we are alive to the uncertain certainty that God is for us, and that our lives are meaningful, that Christ is alive among us, and that he sends us into the world to declare his saving love for all humankind.

But can there be anything wrong, then, with Thomas? Yes. At least as he is represented here, Thomas can be regarded as the patron saint of biblical literalism or biblical fundamentalism, on the one hand, and of much present-day atheism, on the other. The two, you know, *are twins* (as Thomas was said to be a "twin"), and they are born of the belief that for anything to be held to be *true* it must be verified by sense perception (touch, sight, etc.) and its more sophisticated version, scientific experimentation, because on this way of looking at things *material reality exhausts and defines all reality*.

The one twin asserts that, because I have felt the mark of the nails, and because I have seen a physical body I can believe that Jesus is risen from the dead and can assert that he is God and will save me ("My Lord and my God!"). The other twin asserts that, since these stories are clearly myths and that there is no evidence that a dead man came back to physical life, and there is *every evidence* that this *cannot* occur, Jesus was *not* risen from the dead, was *not* the Son of God, and that, what's more, there cannot be a God.

Both twins assume that this-worldly, material reality is all there is. So the fundamentalist assumes that God must be an ordinary being who can sometimes perform magical tricks and can do ordinary things in an extraordinary way. The new atheist says, "No, that cannot be. Look around you. All you see is 'nature red in tooth and claw' and different mobs of angry, hostile, and repressive religious people."

To both of them the risen Christ—the symbol of God, the personal whole of reality in whom "we live and move and have our being"—says "blessed are those who have not seen and yet have faith." That is, you *know* that reality is big, bigger than the material world; you *know* that God is "love divine, all loves excelling" and that Christ re-presents this same God-for-us. Christ *is* alive. Seeing is *not* believing; rather, experiencing the reality of love is. God is good and our lives are hid with Christ in God.

I have written a more measured and reasonable account of religion ("Religion through My Eyes"), but I think it is time to stop and engage in some discussion.

4

RELIGION THROUGH MY EYES

MY CONCEPT OF RELIGION AND HOW I UNDERSTAND MY RELIGIOUS BELIEFS AND PRACTICES

(This talk was originally given at
Temple Emanu el for Rabbi Dan Roberts)
1999
David R. Mason

Whenever I reflect on the phenomenon of religion in general or the plurality of different religions among the variety of human cultures, I find it helpful to distinguish religions themselves from a more basic dimension of human existence of which the religions give symbolic expression. At present I tend to name this more fundamental level of human existence "faith," although I am not wedded to this term. I recognize that "faith" is often used to designate other quite different phenomena. For instance, faith is frequently taken to mean "blind faith," or an attitude that is opposed to reason, rather than a deeper dimension of the human spirit that gives rise to and directs reason and other noble human faculties. "Faith," when used in this sense, is a low level of intellect that delights in accepting propositions about the world even when, or especially when, they run counter to reasonable argument and evidence. It is characterized as "the schoolboy's definition of faith": "Faith is when you believe something that you know ain't true."[1] This most definitely is what I *do not* mean.

---

1. James, *The Will to Believe and Other Essays in Popular Philosophy*, 29.

I also recognize that "faith" is often used simply as a cognate for "religion," as when we speak of "interfaith dialogue" or "the great faiths of the world." OK. These are what I call "religions."

What I mean by this underlying something-or-other that we all have in common is a deep and, I believe, ineradicable confidence that existence is finally worthwhile; it is a trust that life is ultimately meaningful and that all my acts and experiences are "something that matters."[2] We are not isolated or separated from one another; we are related, and our acts affect others. Nor are our acts and experiences effaced, wiped out, brought to nothing. They matter, they are etched indelibly into the face of the universe, they are "written into the Book of Life." This basic trust in the meaningfulness of existence, I think, is given with human existence; it is part of what it means to be human, and it is all but instinctive; it is almost what Santayana called "[a]nimal faith being a sort of expectation . . . earlier than in tuition."[3]

Of course I know that there is much to challenge this basic confidence: things go awry; bad things *do* happen to good people; there are unspeakable tragedies, people suffer wrongfully and immeasurably; many are born into obscene poverty and injustice—"the slings and arrows of outrageous fortune"—while others seem well situated (but even in the best of circumstances relationships often go sour and projects seem to come to naught, and sometimes despair takes over). I am aware of suicides and "lives of quiet desperation." Yet in the teeth of all this I sense that even a grumble, a dulled stare, a suicide is made with an all but unconscious sense that it *makes a difference* somehow, somewhere. Albert Camus, the French literary genius who is supposed to have championed "the absurd," and was thought by some to advocate nihilism, expressed the logic of my conviction. He said: "The absurd can be considered only as a point of departure," for "a literature of despair is a contradiction in terms. How can one limit oneself to the idea that nothing has sense and that we must despair of everything? . . . In the same way that there is no absolute materialism, since merely in order to fashion this word it is already necessary to say that there is something in this world more than matter, there is no total nihilism. From the moment one says that all is nonsense, one expresses something which has sense."[4]

Even so, most of us do not remain poised at this basic level of implicit trust in the worth of our lives; as I have said we are rudely brought up short by

2. Whitehead, *Modes of Thought*, 159.
3. Santayana, *Scepticism and Animal Faith*, 107.
4. Camus, "The Riddle," 85.

failure, tragedy, suffering, injustice, the transience of life—"mais òu sont les neiges d'antan?"—death. The negativities we daily encounter call into question our basic confidence. And, in fact, in every culture that I am aware of the fundamental way this challenge is met is by *representing* the elemental confidence in symbolic forms that trigger the imagination, tap the well-springs of that original confidence itself, and let it pour forth as hope, joy—religion.

Whitehead, I believe, captured something of the spirit of religion and of this essence when he said: "Religion is the vision of something which stands beyond, behind, and within the passing flux of immediate things; something which is real, and yet waiting to be realized; something which is a remote possibility, and yet the greatest of present facts; something that gives meaning to all that passes, and yet eludes apprehension; something whose possession is the final good, and yet is beyond all reach; something which is the ultimate ideal, and the hopeless quest . . . Apart from [the religious vision] human life is a flash of occasional enjoyments, lighting up a mass of pain and misery, a bagatelle of transient experience."[5]

But, of course, I believe we are never *wholly* apart from that vision or what gives rise to it. And, on the other hand, this vision itself is never expressed in a pure, nonhistorical form. Religions are, inevitably, culturally-bound, historically-relativized expressions of a people's particular way of experiencing and reformulating the basic human confidence that life is something that matters, and then of ordering the lives of people according to the precepts derived from their particular expression of that underlying faith.

Any religion, whether relatively primitive or very advanced, is actually a complex cultural institution and comprises many elements. Among these are: ritual, myth, some vision of the ultimate order of things, a set of subsidiary beliefs, a range of emotions, a code of behavior, and an organizational structure. All of these elements are bound together by a rich set of symbols. The cultural anthropologist Clifford Geertz tried to express this briefly with this definition: "A religion is a system of symbols which acts to establish powerful, pervasive, and long-lasting moods and motivations in men by formulating conceptions of a general order of existence and clothing these conceptions with such an aura of factuality that the moods and motivations seem uniquely realistic."[6]

Let me try to unpack this definition a bit. The "conceptions of a general order of existence" of which he speaks stand for, or express, that *something*

---

5. Whitehead, *Science and the Modern World*, 267–68.
6. Geertz, *The Interpretation of Cultures*, 90.

that Whitehead said "stands beyond, behind, and within the passing flux of immediate things." It is that about the universe that *abides* and yet "gives meaning to all that passes." It is deemed *real*, because as the pragmatist James said, "anything is real of which we find ourselves obliged to take account in any way."[7] At the same time it is waiting to be realized; hence it is the ideal that lures us forward. It is what we take to be the objective correlate of our faith or trust that what we do matters. But this conception has to be "clothed with an aura of factuality." Hence, stories, myths, rituals that reinforce the vision. Beliefs and doctrines, too, give concrete expression to this fundamental worldview. And whether we are looking at myths or rituals or theology, all are expressed with symbols taken from our particular experience, but that point beyond the ordinary to the sacred. These symbols help to establish what Geertz calls "powerful, pervasive, and long-lasting moods and motivations." I take it that he means by "moods" the attitudes and aesthetic preferences that characterize a particular culture. And by "motivations" I take it he refers to the ethical norms that govern behavior and urge us to act in certain ways.

It must be evident from all of this that I regard religions—*any* religion—as historically conditioned, as a *product* of the culture in which it arises. It seems clear that the language in which the beliefs are expressed, the stories told, the ethical principles worked out, are all culturally rooted. So are all symbols and social structures. Thus, any religion is inevitably rooted in and takes its characteristic expressions from the culture in which it arises and represents and serves. Most of us can readily recognize the historical relativity of religions other than our own. It is the beginning of wisdom, however, to acknowledge the relativity of our own religious expressions, beliefs, and institutions. For, to admit our own cultural relativity, that our religion is only one among the many legitimate expressions of that deeper underlying trust in the meaning and worth of existence, even as we recognize that there is a common faith that lies at the ground of all religions, all human existence, is to eschew idolatry. H. Richard Niebuhr said that "the greatest source of evil in life is the absolutizing of the relative." And he elaborated: "In Christianity [this] takes the form of substituting religion, revelation, church or Christian morality for God."[8] Insofar as we avoid such idolatry we take a step toward trusting the one God who creates and redeems all life, all being.

I have emphasized my belief that religions are *products* of culture, but that is by no means all I want to say. Certainly, I do not think that a religion

---

7. James, *Some Problems in Philosophy*, 101.
8. Niebuhr, *The Meaning of Revelation*, viii–ix.

can be lumped together with all the other cultural institutions. For I believe that religion occupies a unique and indispensable place in the life of any culture. Of course, one might say that institutions such as family or clan, organizations for eking out a living and distributing goods, organizations established to defend the group, are equally indispensable. But religion is unique in that it is the most comprehensive of all the cultural institutions; it touches every aspect of human life, it orders the emotions and guides the behavior. As such religion is the treasurehouse of that culture's living symbols and the agency for celebrating and enacting its deepest values. Deeper than this, even, religion raises ever anew and addresses the primary human question, the question about the meaning and worth of life: What is it all about and what must we do about it?

Thus, religion is the chief instrument for expressing and promulgating a culture's fundamental worldview, and in doing so it *creates new cultural expressions*. It is a *producer* as well as a product. For the religion occupies the chief place in articulating the principles that coordinate the worldview with the practical lives—public as well as private—of the members of that culture. It fuses "worldview" and "ethos" by grounding our "ought" in a fundamental "is." Religion coordinates and synthesizes the various disparate elements of a living people and so stamps their history as a unique and significant culture. As I say, we must see religion not simply as a product but also as a producer of a living tradition.

What is more, any religion, in a sense, transcends its own culture. For, even as it gathers together into one unified expression the divers elements of that culture, religion also seeks to give expression to that invariant faith that lies beneath all cultures. But insofar as it does symbolize that which transcends all cultures, or as we might also say, lies at the ground of all being, it is bound to come into conflict with particular cultural expressions, especially when they claim finality for themselves. There is always a powerful element of judgment when the universal touches the particular. So religion must give voice to the *prophetic* as well as to the priestly element; it convicts as well as completes human life.

Yet when all this is taken into account we can say that religion is the chief cultural expression in symbol, myth, ritual, doctrine, and ethics of the ineradicable trust that existence is after all meaningful and that life is "something that matters" infinitely. Despite the innumerable evils that rise up to thwart this trust, religion answers with the confidence that there is that about the changing world that abides. And, therefore, religion *reassures* us that what we do *counts*—it matters. Metaphorically, we might say that our deeds, our joys and sorrows, etch lines in the face of the universe. Since this abiding reality is at the ground and end of all action and experience we can call it a circumambient reality of which we are all parts; it is ever there, yet it is ever changed by what we do.

In speaking thus I have obviously begun to show the influence of my own peculiar religious outlook. To speak of the abiding element as that "circumambient reality of which we are all parts" and to suggest that it is at the beginning and end of all our days as the ultimate (but *not* the *only*) creator and redeemer, and so interacts with all its parts in a *personal* way (it not only abides, but it *cares*)—as the personal whole of which we are all cells or experiences—is to show a *theistic bias*.

Theistic religions, whose great examples are Judaism, Christianity, and Islam, all stake their claim upon a prior assumption that God is personal, that God cares deeply and passionately about the people of God, that God not only acts, but can be worshiped and so is acted upon: God is taken as One who interacts as only a supremely personal, social individual can do.

The non-theistic religions, such as Hinduism, Buddhism, Confucianism, Taoism, and Shinto, doubtless witness to the conviction that there is that about the universe that abides. Thus they all bear witness to the underlying faith that sustains us, and in their own culturally conditioned way they embody a type of authentic human existence.

Even so, I cannot but speak from within a theistically formed culture that understands that the circumambient reality not only abides but cares. To speak specifically to my Jewish friends and, to speak colloquially, we are different "brand name" products but are "generically" the same. This means, so I take it, that the ultimate reality that is internally related to every creature as its ultimate creative source and as the ultimate redemptive end—its Whence and its Whither—is none other than: the loving God of the Jews, decisively known as their liberator from slavery in Egypt, and as the source of Torah that orders the life of every Jew and of Israel, but also the One whose steadfast and compassionate love, proclaimed by the prophets, chastens Israel and yet will never abandon her, never let her go, the God who is there at creation and breathes spirit into humans, the God who is disclosed as the *only* God and to whom all the nations—not only Israel—may return, the God who is the anchor of hope.

That is, of course, merely to highlight the major points and to skip over and miss much of the rich texture of the whole Jewish story. You know that better than I. The point I wish to emphasize, however, is that the God I think I know through that part of the tradition we share—the Hebrew Scriptures—is an intensely personal being, the personal being, the personal whole of which we are all parts, whose transcendence is not separation from us, but is understood in terms of *universal* interaction and who, therefore, is the redeemer of *all* creatures, not just of Israel or of Christians.

Now this same God is re-presented decisively to me as a Christian in and through Jesus, a Jew put to death by Roman officials, but who thereby is known powerfully as the God of suffering love; God is known and worshiped as "the great companion—the fellow-sufferer who understands."[9] I use the verb, "re-presented," because I am convinced that it is central to the Christian story to claim that the God known decisively to us in Jesus is the One who is creatively and redemptively *present to every creature*. As Schubert Ogden, a theologian who has influenced me in understanding the meaning of "Christ" and in countering claims for Christian exclusivism, says: "The claim 'only in Jesus Christ' must be interpreted to mean, not that God acts to redeem in the history of Jesus and in no other history, but that the only God who redeems any history—*although he in fact redeems every history*—is the God whose redemptive action is decisively re-presented in the word that Jesus speaks and is."[10]

This, too, is an overbrief statement, since Christianity from the New Testament days to the present has woven a rich and many textured tapestry. And I will be happy to discuss any of the strands, good or bad, that I know about. But that is the heart of the matter. And to respond adequately is to worship God with the totality of our being. In the words Jesus borrowed directly from Deuteronomy, it is to "love the Lord your God with all your heart, and with all your soul, and with all your might" (Deut 6:5). And Jesus intuitively knew that to "love God" with all our being is "to love your neighbor as yourself" (Lev 19:18). The parable of the "Good Samaritan" (Luke 10:29–37) makes clear that our "neighbor" is *anyone* in need, and the parable of the "King who comes in Judgment" (Matt 25:31–46) makes clear that to do good or bad to the least of creatures is to do it unto God.

Christianity is a religion, historically produced, and as such, has its great store of myths, symbols, ritual, traditions, doctrines, its derivative ethical principles, and organizations. Like every great historical religion it has its subsets or strands. I have grown up in that brand of Christianity marked

---

9. Whitehead, *Process and Reality*, 351.
10. Ogden, *The Reality of God*, 173.

with a special English character, the Episcopal Church, which is Anglicanism transplanted into American, rather democratic, soil. To the consternation of many of my Christian friends we insist that we are *both* Catholic *and* Protestant. We have bishops and priests and love "sacramental worship" and tradition, but we simply do not acknowledge the Bishop of Rome, the Pope, as supreme authority, and we believe that many of the traditions that grew up around the papacy—and many other medieval traditions—are divisive and harmful. And we cherish "the freedom of a Christian."[11]

Anglicans make their appeal to validate their religious experience to the *Bible* and to the long theological and ecclesiastical *tradition*, but also to *reason* and to *conscience* or the working of God in the non-rational parts of the soul. They believe that too exclusive a reliance on any one of these is bound to distort the reception of the religious message. Thus we think we are rooted in the *biblical* tradition and in the great *tradition* of Christianity through the centuries, but also are very attentive to the voice of *reason* and not insensitive to the deeper stirrings of God's *Spirit* in our times. I suspect that the best in every religious tradition would make similar claims.

But, of course, my own way of trying to embody these principles is colored by the tradition that began anew in England in the sixteenth century. In a day when pluralism is rampant, and each group is increasingly aware of its own identity almost in opposition to others, I am, I hope, increasingly aware of my share in the common humanity, a child of God. But I am not unmindful of, nor unappreciative of, the way English culture has shaped my own religious response. My plea, to myself and to others, is that, while we should enjoy and relish the enriching aspects of our particular culture, we be honest enough to hear about its shortcomings and that we *not* "absolutize the relative." The more we're aware of others and their own grounding in God, the less likely that is to be. In that spirit I end with another quote from my favorite philosopher: "Evil is the brute motive force of fragmentary purpose, disregarding the eternal vision. Evil is overruling, retarding, hurting. The power of God is the worship He inspires. That religion is strong which in its ritual and its modes of thought evokes an apprehension of the commanding vision. The worship of God is not a rule of safety—it is an adventure of the spirit, a flight after the unattainable. The death of religion comes with the repression of the high hope of adventure."[12]

---

11. Luther, "The Freedom of a Christian," *Three Treatises*, 265–316.
12. Whitehead, *Science and the Modern World*, 268–69.

5

THE ROOTS OF ANTISEMITISM IN THE GOSPELS

2002
David R. Mason

I want you to know that everything that I have to say to you about the roots of anti-Semitism in Christian literature and history is said as a committed Christian. I am convinced, however, that it is a very real part of that "freedom [for which] Christ has set us free" (Gal 5:1) to face squarely the negative facts that are a part of our heritage. And, if we are to get at the foundation of all subsequent negative Christian attitudes toward Jews we must go to the New Testament, particularly the Gospels.

I say go to the Gospels, because I believe they contain the most, and the most virulent, anti-Jewish diatribes, slurs, and accusations in the New Testament. Even so, let us pause briefly to consider the apostle Paul. Paul undoubtedly played a major role in transforming the Christian movement from a Jewish sect into a religion to be contended with in the Western world. Yet he has lately had a pretty bad press. He is often accused of being a misogynist (although I think there is less evidence for this than is alleged) and some people believe, as did my favorite philosopher, Alfred North Whitehead, that "the man who . . . did more than anybody else to distort and subvert Christ's teaching was Paul."[1]

No doubt, because Paul is well known for having insisted that people are "justified [or made right with God] by *faith apart from* works prescribed by the *Torah*" (Rom 3:28), many people think he has a special animosity

---

1. Price, *Dialogues of Alfred North Whitehead*, 307.

toward the religion of his birth. But a careful reading of his letters shows this not to be the case. Paul is argumentative and irascible at times, especially so when dealing with certain followers of Christ who wanted to make obedience to Jewish prescriptions a prerequisite for faith in Christ, but he is rarely anti-Jewish and even, at times, boasts of his Jewish heritage (e.g., 2 Cor 11:22 and Phil 3:5). Typically, Paul wants to proclaim the good news that God's power for salvation is available to *everyone* irrespective of their religious or cultural background. As he says, salvation is available "to everyone who has faith, to the Jew first, and also to the Greek," by which he means "Jews and everyone else," for as he goes on to say, "God shows no partiality" (Rom 1:16, 2:11).

There is one place, I admit, where Paul falls prey to the tendency to blame the Jews for Christ's death: in the First Letter to the Thessalonians he says, "For you suffered the same things from your own countrymen as they did from the Jews, who killed both the Lord Jesus and the prophets, and drove us out, and displease God and oppose everyone by hindering us from speaking to the Gentiles" (1 Thess 2:14–15). I bring up this one plainly negative claim by Paul because, although I do not think it is at all typical of him, it is expressive of an early family quarrel that breaks out into irrational anger and is, also, a forerunner of the gospel claims.

Before we take up the drumbeat of anti-Jewish claims in the Gospels I need to take note of several historical facts and observations. First, all of the Gospels are agreed that Jesus' death was by *crucifixion*, which was the *Roman* government's form of capital punishment. Scholars disagree as to how much influence the Jewish Sanhedrin and Temple priests *may* have had, but at most two hundred Jews out of four or five million living at the time would have had a hand in bringing Jesus to crucifixion. But we should not make a leap from one or *a few* to *all*. We never, for instance, say, "*Americans* killed John Kennedy" nor do we say, "*Southerners* killed Abraham Lincoln." And it would be improper, and even unjust, to say, "*Romans* or *Italians* killed Jesus." Even so, as we will see, the Gospels first declare a growing animosity between Jesus and the Pharisees, and then the other Jewish leaders, and then "the people," and finally, "the Jews." Ultimately the claim is that the *Jews* are responsible for Jesus' death. And to this the Gospel of Matthew adds, after declaring Pilate's innocence: "All the people answered, 'His blood be on us *and on our children!*'" (Matt 27:25).

Another observation, grounded in the historical-critical study of the Gospels, is that none of the Gospels is an eyewitness account of the historical

THE ROOTS OF ANTISEMITISM IN THE GOSPELS

Jesus. Indeed, the Gospels are not even an attempt to record the biography of Jesus; they are proclamations of good news about Jesus as the Christ—perhaps "theological novellas"—rather than biographies. All were written in the last third of the first century, and all the gospel writers were editors and creative writers, but not, strictly speaking, reporters. They were people who fashioned quite different accounts from stories and sayings that circulated for several generations among the earliest Christian communities. Some of the sayings circulated without any narrative framework, while other sayings and stories were found embedded in liturgies, preaching, and controversies with local Jewish congregations. The gospel writers synthesized these diverse stories and sayings into a new whole, creating sequences and situations, and even placing words in the mouth of Jesus. John is the most highly theological and the least historically reliable, but all the Gospels must be regarded as narrative theology rather than as biographical record. Inevitably, all of them reflect the times and situations in which they were written. Thus, with respect to the anti-Jewish passages, which bear witness to tensions that had arisen between two fragile groups—the followers of Jesus and the scattered Jews led by the Pharisees—in the Roman Empire in the years following the Jewish revolt of 66–70 CE, one is bound to agree with a modern Jewish commentator: "The anti-Jewish Jesus who emerges from the gospels is thus the product of writers who conceptualized him in the light of what had become their own anti-Jewish orientation, often a function in turn of whatever such views were current among their own constituencies . . . It is vital that modern readers of the gospels come to understand that the historical Jesus and the Jesus of the gospels are simply not one and the same. Reminiscent of a painting overlaid by later retouchings . . . what we have in the gospels is one Jesus-image superimposed upon another."[2]

Whether, or to what extent, anyone can penetrate the layers to attempt to form an accurate picture of the historical Jesus is still very much in debate. What is certain, though, is that whatever emerges will be fragmentary: perhaps a teacher and healer who proclaimed the imminence of God's reign and associated himself with its advent, a Jew who gathered disciples and was put to death by the Roman government.

The next historical observation is that Mark is the earliest of the Gospels to have been written, probably around the time of the Jewish revolt against Rome and Rome's siege and sacking of Jerusalem and the

---

2. Cook, "The New Testament: Confronting Its Impact on Jewish-Christian Relations," *Introduction to Jewish-Christian Relations*, 55.

destruction of the Temple (ca. 68–70 CE). Matthew and Luke come about a generation later, and both make use of Mark but add other material and "sayings" of Jesus. The Gospel of John, which paints quite a different picture of Jesus' life than do the other three, comes a bit later. John is the least historically reliable, and the most venomous in attacking the Jews.

But, in fact, all four Gospels are much more highly theological than they are historically accurate. Mark, for instance, wants to make the point that Jesus' suffering and death is part of God's providence as carried out by the chief priests and scribes. Even so, he portrays Jesus' disciples as increasingly failing him and falling away by not grasping the point that he "came not to be served, but to serve and to give his life as a ransom for many." Matthew wants to show that in the early part of his ministry Jesus was favored by the crowds, but about half way through (chapter 13), because of growing animosity, Jesus *turns away* from the crowds and directs his teaching mainly to his disciples (although, as we will see, he takes time out to denounce the scribes and Pharisees). Luke always wants to claim that Jesus "fulfills the Scripture" so that his death and resurrection are in fulfillment of the Law and the Prophets. John proclaims God's Word and God's pure unbounded love incarnate in Christ, but struggles to square this with his animosity toward the Jews. Nevertheless, all four Gospels accede to the public fact that the Roman procurator, Pontius Pilate, had Jesus put to death however much they may want to place the blame elsewhere.

So let us take up the Gospels, more or less in the order in which they were written. Mark is the least vituperative toward the Jews, but still he portrays Jesus as at odds with scribes and Pharisees over matters of the Torah observation and blasphemy (plucking grain on the Sabbath, forgiving sins, etc.). Moreover, from time to time in Mark the people oppose Jesus. Even the people of his own town "took offense at him." Interestingly, toward the end of his life Jesus is portrayed by Mark as at odds with the chief priests of the Temple and the scribes, and Jesus "predicts" the destruction of the Temple (because this was probably written shortly after, or immediately before the destruction, it is highly likely that such a "prediction" was written backward by "Mark"). The night before Jesus' death "crowds of people" came along with Judas with swords and clubs. Moreover, Mark tries to exonerate Pilate, laying the blame for the decision for Jesus' death on the crowds of Jewish people: "Pilate, wishing to satisfy the crowds ... delivered [Jesus] to be crucified" (Mark 15:15). So, despite Mark's theology, which maintained that Jesus' death was part of God's plan, and despite the obvious historical fact that the Roman imperial authority in charge put Jesus to death, Mark somehow tries to lay the blame for Jesus' death on the chief priests, scribes, and the crowds, with the Pharisees lurking in the background.

Matthew ups the ante considerably. In addition to taking over much of Mark's account of Jesus' public life, Matthew portrays Jesus in chapter 13 as turning away from the crowds (the Jewish people), because of a growing animosity. There are several conflicts with Pharisees culminating with a whole set of diatribes in chapter 23—the famous "woe to you scribes and Pharisees" against "scribes and Pharisees." These are said by Jesus to be "hypocrites" who lock people out of the kingdom of heaven and "blind guides who bind people to the law" or "strain at a gnat and swallow a camel," who are "whitewashed tombs," which look beautiful on the outside but are full of the bones of the dead, who are a "brood of vipers" who have killed prophets and wise men. Whereupon, Jesus begins to weep for *Jerusalem* because that city has "killed the prophets." Under the guise of compassion could anything be more libelous?

There could, of course, be other and different ways of portraying the Jews badly. Luke (in 11:37—22:1) reproduces some of the diatribes against the Pharisees that Matt 23 has, although here it is not quite as bad. Notice, however, that in the much beloved parable of the Good Samaritan the priests and Levites are made out to lack compassion. Moreover, Luke has Jesus warn his disciples of times when they will be "brought before synagogues, the rulers and authorities" (Luke 12:11). He tells parables of God rejecting his people, the Jews, in favor of Gentiles (Luke clearly pitches his gospel to a Roman audience). Then, in the Acts of the Apostles, which Luke wrote, Peter and Stephen give speeches in which they blame the Jews for killing Jesus and for killing the prophets; thus, the Jews are constantly portrayed as villains.

But, if Matthew, Mark, and Luke (called the "Synoptic Gospels") build up a case for enmity between Jesus and Pharisees and scribes, and later chief priests and Levites, and finally all the people, culminating with placing the blame for Jesus' death on the people (and in one place "on their children"), the most overtly anti-Jewish gospel is John. It is in this gospel that "the Jews," as a group, are portrayed as the adversaries of Jesus, who himself often seems not to be a Jew at all. The term "the Jews" is used seventy-one times in John, as opposed to a total of sixteen in all the Synoptic Gospels taken together. The term is often used in plainly negative, even hostile, contexts. Let me give a few examples: "The Jews murmured at him because he said, 'I am the bread of life'" (6:41); "The Jews took up stones to stone him" (10:31); "This was why the Jews persecuted Jesus because he [healed a man] on the Sabbath" and "This was why the Jews sought all the more to kill him" (5:16, 18); or, again, "After this Jesus went about Galilee; he would not go about Judea because the Jews sought to kill him" (7:1). All of this comes to a head when "the Jews" cry out to Pilate: "Away with him, away with him, crucify him! . . . We have no king but Caesar" (19:15).

As Eldon Epp, a world-renowned New Testament scholar at Case Western Reserve University, and himself a Christian, says: "When a reader has finished all 21 chapters of John's gospel, the term, 'the Jews,' has been heated by the fire of narrative controversy between Jesus and 'the Jews,' has been hammered by its vehement repetition, and has been forged by the bitter and hostile contexts of many of its occurrences into a red-hot spear, which not only has pierced the side of the Lord of the Church, but now seems menacing also to the Gentile readers of this Christian account of the gospel . . . Imagine the impression made upon Gentile Christians from the second century on by a gospel that speaks repeatedly of 'the Jews' as the persecutors and murderers of Jesus Christ the Lord of the Church."[3]

Anyone who is not profoundly disturbed, even shaken, by the virulent anti-Jewishness of the Gospel of John should, at the very least, try the experiment of reading it as if he or she were a Jew—one whose people have been persecuted at the hands of Christians down through the centuries. I have tried this and have concluded that the remark of a rabbi in 1905 rings true: that John's is the "gospel of Christian love and Jew[ish] hatred."[4] This is all the more troubling because John's Gospel has been the most popular of Christian writings, readily translated, and the source of many easily memorized passages. Indeed, it contains much that is spiritually and theologically profound. Unfortunately, the effect of this has been to suggest that the anti-Jewishness that pervades it is part and parcel of the gospel of God's redemptive love rather than what it is: a historical aberration rooted in the unusually bitter Christian-Jewish relations of the late first century.

Of course, one might well ask whether the animus is all one-sided. Are there no Jewish attacks upon Christians? Apparently, the Pharisees at Jamnia issued a *Benediction against Heretics* in the late first century that

---

3. Epp, "Anti-Semitism and the Popularity of the Fourth Gospel in Chrstianity," *Central Conference of American Rabbis Journal*, 40–41.

4. Kaufmann Kohler, *Jewish Encyclopedia* cited in Epp, "Anti-Semitism and the Popularity of the Fourth Gospel," 49.

THE ROOTS OF ANTISEMITISM IN THE GOSPELS

condemned both "Nazarenes" and "heretics."[5] There may have been others. My only point here, however, is that the later negative attitude of Christians toward Jews is rooted in the Gospels.

Indeed, the animus against the Jews that is so evident in John's Gospel took root and grew as Christianity became more and more a religion of the Roman Empire. As one observer put it: "When the western world accepted Christianity Caesar conquered."[6] And the Caesar who did so was Constantine, who claimed to have seen a cross in the sky with the words, "in this sign you will conquer" (*In hoc signo vinces*—a slogan used by the Knights Templar *and* Pall Mall cigarettes!) before he won the battle of Milvian Bridge. Thereupon, the cross, the Roman instrument of death, was transformed into a sword with which to subjugate others. Most of the "others" were Jews scattered throughout the empire.

One of the Christian leaders who early on (mid-fourth century) attacked the Jews in the name of Christ and justified killing them was *Saint John Chrysostom*, the Bishop of Antioch. In a series of sermons he denounced Jews as whores, wild animals, drunkards, worse than animals marked for slaughter—enemies of Christ. Indeed, he is said to have said of the Jews, "When animals are unfit for work, they are marked for slaughter, and this is the very thing the Jews have experienced. By making themselves unfit for work, they have become ready for slaughter. This is why Christ said, 'As for my enemies who did not want me to reign over them, bring them here and slay them before me.'"[7] After these sermons there were violent outbursts against the Jews with the synagogues in Antioch destroyed. A half-century later in Alexandria there was the first large-scale pogrom, which destroyed the entire Jewish community there.

Thence it goes: from preacher to pope to passion plays to Luther to Shakespeare, culminating in the Holocaust. Institutions and the mindset of common folk were formed and colored with a distinct anti-Jewish animus whose roots are to be found in the New Testament, especially the *Gospels*.

I am convinced, however, that the anti-Jewish sentiment so clearly evident in the Gospels is an aberration contrary to *the gospel*: the good news that "God was in Christ reconciling the world to Godself" (2 Cor 5:19), and that the various New Testament witnesses to Jesus are so many ways of attempting to confess that Jesus, by his manner of life, his teaching, and his

---

5. See Harris, *New Testament*, 52.
6. Whitehead, *Process and Reality*, 342.
7. Carroll, *Constantine's Sword*, 213.

death decisively *represents* "the power of God for salvation to *everyone* who has faith, to the Jew first and also to the Greek" (Rom 1:16). That is to say, God and divine redemptive love are always, already present and available to everyone; Jesus does not exclusively constitute God-in-the-world, nor are Christians alone the redeemed. As Schubert Ogden has so powerfully and carefully said: "The claim 'only in Jesus Christ' must be interpreted to mean, not that God acts to redeem only in the history of Jesus and in no other history, but that the only God who redeems any history—*although he in fact redeems every history*—is the God whose redemptive action is decisively re-presented in the word that Jesus speaks and is."[8] If we are to be loyal to this gospel we will be able to recognize and bring to light what is hateful and harmful in any part of holy Scripture and be strong and free enough to see it for what it is, a deviation from the gospel: "Jesus said to the Jews who had believed in him [presumably his *Jewish* followers] 'If you continue in my word, you are truly my disciples, and *you will know the truth and the truth will make you free*'" (John 8:31–32).

---

8. Ogden, *The Reality of God*, 173.

6

THE STATUS OF GOD-TALK

David R. Mason
John Carroll University
December 6, 1976

(On November 19, 1976 *The Carroll News*, the student newspaper of John Carroll University, published an exchange between Professor Thomas Tomasic and me regarding the meaninglessness or the significance of any talk about "God." We then agreed to a public debate. The following is the talk that I gave as part of that debate.)

I wish to thank the editorial staff of *The Carroll News* for publishing the exchange between Professor Tomasic and me and for promoting this public debate. And I wish to thank my good friend, Tom Tomasic, for bringing both his good will and clear thought to this discussion.

It seems evident to me that, if we are to shed any light on the "status of God-talk," we need to establish the meaning of the object in question, namely, God. It is notoriously true that the term "God," or cognates, has been applied to nearly every imaginable object, from stones to elderly, bearded gentlemen to sheer abstractions. Yet, if we are seriously to discuss the "adequate object of religious attitudes"[1] we must exclude from consideration all lesser candidates for deity and fix our attention on the idea of that which can be worshiped by any creature whatever without reservation and without contradiction. The adequate object of the religious attitude is that which is supremely worthy of worship. This would be the "supreme being"

---

1. Findlay, "Can God's Existence Be Disproved?," in *New Essays in Philosophical Theology*, 47.

or the "perfect being" or, in Anselm's precise phrase, "a being than which nothing greater can be conceived."

Now, this may not seem to have taken us very far in our search for the reference range of the concept God, but I think that the difficulty, if any, is with the abstract character and the ambiguity of the phrase "that than which nothing greater can be conceived." Whatever its difficulties, if we reflect on this we can see that it rules out everything less than a perfect being. Moreover, we may take another step with Anselm—a giant step indeed—toward narrowing the range of possible meanings attaching to perfection or the concept of deity. It was Anselm's intuition, to which he first gave voice in the third chapter of the *Proslogion* and then repeatedly in his reply to his first critic, the monk Gaunilo, that, properly understood, the perfect being *cannot exist contingently*. This is to say that the perfect being cannot be something that might not exist or, if it exists, came into being and might cease to exist, or depends for its existence on something else. Therefore, "perfection"—or "that than which nothing greater can be conceived"—cannot be applied literally to islands (Gaunilo's example), dollars (Kant), or anything that might not exist, or might cease existing, or does not as yet exist but might begin to exist. Perfection, understood in a theistic context, means at the very least "*that which cannot be conceived not to exist.*"

This is an essential point to make if we are to focus our attention on the theistic concept of God. And yet it is a point that critic and believer alike often ignore or throw away. And so, at the risk of offending you with repetition, I shall lay out several of Anselm's statements and, then, attempt to clarify them in coming to grips with a concept of God that is cognitively significant in the present context.

In the third chapter of *Proslogion* Anselm argues that "if that, than which nothing greater can be conceived, can be conceived not to exist, it is not that than which nothing greater can be conceived . . . There is, then, so truly a being than which nothing greater can be conceived to exist, that it cannot even be conceived not to exist."[2] Clearly, here Anselm is establishing the point that perfection, if it is understood aright, cannot exist contingently; it cannot be such that it "can be conceived not to exist," since it is greater to exist in the mode of necessity ("that which cannot be conceived not to exist"). Again, in his reply to Gaunilo, who had sought to discredit Anselm's reasoning by reducing it to the specious argument from the idea of something to its reality (Gaunilo's example: I can conceive of a "perfect

2. Anselm, *St. Anselm*, 8–9.

island" but this in no way assures its existence in reality), Anselm insisted on differentiating the type or mode of existence of God (*necessary existence*) and the reasoning applicable to it, from all other types of ordinary or contingent existence and the reasoning applicable to them. For example, he mentions several types of what we would call "contingent existence": (a) "whatever at any place or time does not exist as a whole, even if it is existent"; (b) "whatever can be conceived to exist and does not exist"; (c) one's own existence, which, although it is indubitable at the present, nevertheless is such that it can be conceived not to exist.[3]

In sharp distinction from these types of existence Anselm sets "that than which a greater is inconceivable" as "without beginning or end," and as "existing always and everywhere as a whole," and finally as that "alone [of which] it can be said that it is impossible to conceive of his non-existence."[4] Yet he insists again that "whatever exists, except that being than which a greater cannot be conceived, can be conceived not to exist."[5] Thus Anselm distinguishes all that we call ordinary or contingent existence, on the one hand, from what is called necessary existence or that whose nonexistence is logically impossible, on the other hand. And it is this latter *alone* to which Anselm's argument applies. And so he says: "Now I promise confidently that if any man shall devise anything existing either in reality or in concept alone (*except that than which a greater cannot be conceived*) to which he can adapt the sequence of my reasoning, I will discover that thing, and will give him his lost island not to be lost again."[6] (Anselm's *Reply to Gaunilo*, as well as chapter 4 of *Proslogion* are usually passed over or ignored by the critics) The point is that all attempts to refute Anselm's argument by recourse to illustrations of "islands of the Blest" more excellent than any other country, perfect dollars, and the like are wholly wide of the mark; they do not engage Anselm's argument.

Now why have I dwelt at such great length on the conception and the precise phrasing of the thinker whose body lies in the cathedral at Canterbury? It is not that I find his concept of God to be wholly without fault. Indeed, it may be fairly contended, with J. N. Findlay, that if we accept *everything* that Anselm thought to be contained in the idea of deity then it turns out to be self-contradictory so that what the argument establishes is the

3. Ibid., 155.
4. Ibid., 160–61.
5. Ibid., 160.
6. Ibid., 158.

necessary non-existence of God. A disastrous consequence indeed! Clearly, I do not feel constrained to accept a concept that is the idea of an impossibility. But what is important about Anselm's intuition is that he fixes the reference range for any intelligible discussion of the *existence* of God, and that reference range excludes contingent propositions and empirical proofs and disproofs. Anselm's insight established that it is only metaphysical concepts and necessary propositions that are applicable to deity and that the only kinds of proofs or disproofs that are at all appropriate are strictly logical ones. As Malcolm said: "What Anselm has proved is that the notion of contingent existence or contingent nonexistence cannot have any application to God. His existence must be either logically necessary or logically impossible. The only intelligible way of rejecting Anselm's claim that God's existence is necessary is to maintain that the concept of God, as a being a greater than which cannot be conceived, is self-contradictory or nonsensical."[7]

At this point I wish to recall for you that Professor Tomasic, in his interview with *The Carroll News*, made the revealing assertion that "the problem is not the existential status of God, but lies with our knowledge about God which is supposedly communicated via theological statements." In light of what we have just seen to be the logic of discourse about God, as distinct from that appropriate to all other beings, we see that the problem is *precisely* the "existential status of God." If we are to discuss "God" at all, and not some pseudo-concept, then we must keep in mind that the existential status of that being "than which nothing greater can be conceived" (and about which we are talking) is that of *necessary existence*—or else the logical impossibility of existing at all—and *not* that of ordinary or contingent existence. The existential status of divinity is unique among individuals. In fact, God is that individual alone whose "existence" is said to be logically necessary and not to be discussed in terms of empirically falsifiable propositions—or else "God" applies literally to nothing conceivable. But to claim that the reference range of talk about God is exhausted by what can legitimately be said about finite or contingent things, and to declare, moreover, that "epistemological agnosticism" is the only position available to a religious system having a transcendent God, is to declare ahead of time one's intention *not* to talk about the God of theism. Indeed, Professor Tomasic, like so many others, is confused about the meaning of God (or the "reference range" for talk about God) and the existential status of God.

---

7. Malcolm, "Anselm's Ontological Arguments" in Plantinga, ed., *The Ontological Argument From St. Anselm to Contemporary Philosophers*, 145.

THE STATUS OF GOD-TALK

Now I wish to return to another point. I have, perhaps recklessly, alluded to the possibility that the concept of God as entailing "necessary existence," might turn out to be a self-contradictory concept, which would mean the necessary *nonexistence* or the *impossibility* of the being of whom it was posited. Anselm clearly believed that the idea of "that which cannot be conceived not to exist" made sense and so was not nonsensical or self-contradictory. And, because an actual religion includes this concept as applicable to its proper object, the idea of "necessary existence" itself is not, on the face of it, unthinkable. So I think the burden of proof would fall on those who claim that necessary existence is absurd. I don't think it is.

Despite the fact that the idea of "necessary existence" is not nonsensical, it is apparent that the concept of *God*, as it is often understood by believer and unbeliever alike, includes ideas that are themselves incompatible with one another. Therefore, the concept of God itself appears to be nonsensical; in other words, *this God* would be an impossibility.

For example, sometimes it is said that God is *eternal*, which means literally that God is timeless and wholly without duration; yet, at the same time, it is said that God knows things that *occur in time*, and this knowledge must take place through a duration. Part of the essence of finite things is their very temporality, so that to know them as they are requires knowing them through a duration or temporally (Also, to know entities as "potentially something" is different from knowing them as actually this or that). Hence, there is an incompatibility between God's "eternity" and God's knowledge of temporal things. A similar problem Anselm saw, but did not resolve at all satisfactorily, (*Proslogion*, chapter 7) is in the joining of the assertion of God's complete independence and total immutability with that of God's love or compassion. In the first place, "compassion" means "suffering with," which entails being moved; moreover, any lover is bound to be dependent for the content of the love on the one loved and, insofar, is affected or changed or "moved." Again a conflict: immutability / being moved. To bring us back closer to the issue at hand, the existential modality of God, it is sometimes claimed that God is "wholly necessary." Apparently this means that God is, *in every respect*, eternal, without composition (simple), and without dependence on anything; so not only is God's existence necessary but all God's acts and relations to the world are similarly necessary. But at the same time it is claimed that God "makes a real difference" in the finite, contingent world. But to make a real difference in the contingent world is, by definition, to be subject to empirical falsification (though not inevitably by sense experience) or to be *contingent*. And a being that is wholly necessary and partly contingent is as impossible as a "round square." This is why J. N. Findlay said: "It was indeed an ill day for Anselm when he hit upon his famous proof. For on that day he not only laid bare something that is of the essence of an adequate religious object, but something that entails its necessary non-existence."[8] And so there is something to the claim that, *on a certain way of conceiving God*, God is logically impossible.

What then? Must we "throw in the towel"? No. It is evident, however, that we must examine the God question more carefully than either traditional theology or empirical atheism—or, for that matter, "epistemological agnosticism"—have done. This requires that we consider two important points: the meaning of "necessity" or "necessary" especially with respect to "God"; and the distinction between the "existence" of any individual and its actual "states of existence."

The first step in bringing precision and clarity to our concept is to get straight just what the idea of necessity means and can mean with respect to God. Charles Hartshorne, who has given closer attention to this matter than most philosophers of recent times, points out that the "necessary" is abstract; it is "what all possible states of reality have in common."[9] This means that the absolutely necessary is the abstract residuum common to all things actual or possible. It is what the tradition meant by "being itself," although many in the tradition perplexingly treated "being itself" as an individual worthy of worship. Imagine worshiping an abstraction.

The second step is to get clear the important distinction between *any* being's bare *existence* and its full, concrete *actuality*, or its *states of existence*. The distinction is one we habitually make when thinking of ourselves or other persons. We think of the person as maintaining the same existence throughout his or her lifetime, but we see that the "states of existence" of that person change from moment to moment and the present state of the person is contingent upon various things having occurred.

Now, with respect to the perfect individual, God, necessity means the bare necessity to exist in some state or other no matter what, in fact, comes to pass. Had Anselm been free of his Greek philosophical bias, Hartshorne thinks, he might have seen that "God's necessary existence must be very different from His total concrete or factual reality. The divine necessity is

---

8. Findlay, "Can God's Existence Be Disproved?," in *New Essays in Philosophical Theology*, 55.

9. Hartshorne, *Anselm's Discovery*, 43.

that such abstract traits or 'perfections' as 'knowing all there is to know' must be realized in some form, with respect to some concrete world of knowable things, but not necessarily in the form and with respect to the world which actually obtain."[10] In another place Hartshorne reinforces this view and elaborates it:

> God merely as necessary is less than any contingent thing whatever, even the meanest. To worship the necessary is but a subtle form of idolatry... For God as necessary is God considered under an extreme abstraction, God as barely existing somehow, in some state of concrete actuality or other, no matter what. But God cannot be limited to His merely necessary being; He is the individual that could not fail to be actualized in some contingent particular form. This implies an immeasurable superiority; but what actualized the superiority is God-now, or God-then, not just God at any time or as eternal, which is a mere abstraction. The necessity that there be some contingent actualization is inherent in the unique abstractness of the identifying divine individuality or essence.[11]

I realize that it is difficult to digest all of this, especially on first encountering it. But the point is that "necessary existence" is, indeed, crucial to the definition of the perfect individual. But this means only that God's bare *existence* is unchanging, independent of any contingent occurrence, eternal—in a word, necessary. But this bare necessity, this *thatness*, in no way constitutes all of the concrete individual, God. The situation is analogous to the following: although the genetic identity of the individual, Thomas M. Tomasic, remains constant from birth to death, the concrete states of that individual—Tomasic-then, Tomasic-now—change continuously with his changing relations with the world so that what once was a sweet, cherubic youth has become a learned, if somewhat disputatious philosopher. The relation of *God's (necessary) existence* to God's *states of existence*, the changing actuality that is God-then, God-now, is similar. Although God's mode of existence is radically different than that of any contingent being because it is the mode of necessity and so is literally unchanged and wholly uninfluenced by anything, the divine *actuality* or *states of existence* are similar in that they are influenced, change, and grow. Still, with respect to the states of existence of God, there is a radical difference with any contingent being; whereas all finite beings relate to, influence, and are influenced by but a

---

10. Hartshorne, *Anselm's Discovery*, 48.
11. Ibid., 102.

few others, the divine individual relates to, influences, and is influenced by *all* others.

It is on this understanding of the abstractness of necessity and the concreteness of the perfect individual who necessarily actualizes Godself in some state or other, and only on this understanding, that we can avoid the dilemma of meeting the demands of the religious attitude by positing a self-contradictory concept of God. God's necessity as such does not and cannot make a "real difference" in the contingent world. *That* perfection exists necessarily—a mode totally other than contingent existence—is logically true, but abstract; it is compatible with any state of affairs whatever. *What* the content of perfection is, the actual state of existence of the perfect individual, God, is contingent upon what actually becomes and, in turn, "makes a real difference" in the world.

Here we have an idea of God that is cognitively significant. There is mystery enough in the actual content of the divine life that is, of course, unfathomable. But there is no "mystery"—or, better, contradiction— in the idea of a perfect individual who exists necessarily, but has contingent relations with a contingent, changing world. Divine "transcendence" consists in the logically unique status of divine existence, necessity, together with the universal interaction of the divine actuality. These concepts make sense; they can be discussed. Therefore theology has a future as well as a past.

7

THREE RECENT TREATMENTS OF THE ONTOLOGICAL ARGUMENT

David R. Mason
(*Ohio Journal of Religious Studies* 2, no. 1 [1974] 28–43.)

It has been remarked that to be judged worthy of refutation by succeeding generations of thinkers is a subtle, but very high, form of praise. Such has been the lot of St. Anselm and his famous proof for the existence of God. Beginning with the immediate response by Gaunilo and continuing with that of St. Thomas, the refutations by Hume and Kant, and in our own century those of Russell and others, Anselm's reasoning has come under various kinds of attack. Yet its utter simplicity and brilliance are fascinating, and so in our day we find a resurgence of philosophical and theological interest in the ontological argument.[1]

The following essay treats the arguments of three modern philosophers representing major positions with respect to Anselm's proof: (1) that it decisively *disproves* God's existence; (2) that one form of Anselm's argument does indeed establish God's existence; (3) that if "necessity" attaches to God's total being, the argument leads to God's necessary non-existence or impossibility, but that if "necessary existence" is construed as an aspect of the total concrete actuality, God, then the argument is valid and fruitful. Although our three thinkers—J. N. Findlay, Norman Malcolm, and Charles Hartshorne—reach different conclusions, they are agreed that most of the

---

1. Two recent anthologies offer excellent selections both from the past and the present: Plantinga, ed., *The Ontological Argument*; and Hick and McGill, eds., *The Many-faced Argument*. The latter contains an excellent bibliography.

criticisms of Anselm have not touched the nerve of the argument, namely, the concept of necessary existence. In addition to surveying the three positions, the essay maintains that Hartshorne's position is the most solid with respect both to philosophical and religious demands.

Findlay

In his widely read article, "Can God's Existence Be Disproved?,"[2] J. N. Findlay argues brilliantly that a God who is an "adequate object of the religious attitude" must be "inescapable and necessary." But, he insists, it is "self-evidently absurd" to attribute existence to any necessary concept. The conjunction of "necessity," or that which is logically true and "existence," or that which is factually verifiable—having the "character of 'making a real difference'"—disproves the existence of God. Thus he writes: "It was an ill day for Anselm when he hit upon his famous proof. For on that day he not only laid bare something that is of the essence of an adequate religious object, but something that entails its necessary non-existence."[3]

Findlay's argument is strong and must be taken seriously. It begins with the idea of God as the "adequate object of religious attitudes."[4] The religious attitude, in its broadest sense, is "one in which we tended to abase ourselves before some object, to defer to it wholly, to devote ourselves to it with unquestioning enthusiasm, to bend the knee before it, whether literally or metaphorically."[5] Moreover, in deferring wholly to its object, this attitude presumes some qualities in the object. What are these?

First, the object adequate to religious attitudes plainly is said to have "superiority," and this in such manner that the worshipper feels reduced to "comparative nothingness." But this leads us to the demand that the religious object "should have *unsurpassable* supremacy along all avenues, that it should tower *infinitely* above all other objects."[6] It is unworthy of the object of worship, Findlay insists, to be limited in any way. Next, we are led by the demands of religious adequacy to assert that the object be "all-comprehensive," which means that "there mustn't be anything capable

2. Findlay, "Can God's Existence Be Disproved?," in *New Essays in Philosophical Theology*, 47–56.
3. Ibid., 55.
4. Ibid., 48.
5. Ibid., 49.
6. Ibid., 51.

of existing or displaying any virtue, without owing all of these absolutely to this single source."[7] Finally, the demands of religious adequacy lead us irresistibly to assert that the object possess its qualities "*in some necessary manner.*"[8] No matter how excellent a being might be, if it merely *happened* to possess its excellences, or if we somehow came to participate in them, it would be unworthy of genuine worship.

Now, we should be quite clear as to where Findlay has led us: he sees that the demands of our worship are such that the object of worship must be not only superior to all *actual* beings but superior to all possible beings. "God mustn't merely cover the territory of the actual, but also, with equal comprehensiveness, the territory of the possible . . . His own non-existence must be wholly unthinkable in any circumstances."[9] This mode of existence, which the demands of religious adequacy posit of God, is totally different from ordinary "contingent existence" that all other beings have. It is conceivable that any other being might not have existed or might cease to exist or might exist other than it in fact does, but, according to the proper demands of worship, this is inconceivable of God. His must be "necessary existence."

Furthermore, Findlay sees that the demands of worship do not stop with the bare necessity of God's *existence*, but cover his properties: "Not only is it contrary to the demands and claims inherent in religious attitudes that their object should exist 'accidentally'; it is also contrary to those demands that it should *possess its various excellences* in some merely adventitious or contingent manner."[10] This means that in addition to his necessary existence, God must hold his properties in some necessary manner. He must be not merely "wise, good, powerful and so forth," nor even the wisest, best, and most powerful. God must possess these "various qualities *in some necessary manner.*"[11]

The consequences of these demands, Findlay maintains, are disastrous. For, as he points out, in a "modern view of the matter, necessity in propositions merely reflects our use of words, the arbitrary conventions of language."[12] And by this view "necessity in propositions" does not determine or affect existential actualities or possibilities, which are matters of

7. Ibid., 52.
8. Ibid., 53.
9. Ibid., 52.
10. Ibid.
11. Ibid., 53.
12. Ibid., 54.

contingency. Necessary propositions are analytic and, thus, make no real difference in the world of fact or existence. But the proposition, "God exists," purports to do just that. It attempts "to build bridges between mere abstractions and concrete existence."[13] In other words it attempts to conjoin a being whose very essence must be abstract necessity with concrete, factual existence. To require of necessary existence that which is logically impossible for it seems to argue persuasively for its necessary non-existence. Thus he writes:

> The religious frame of mind seems, in fact, to be in a quandary; it seems invincibly determined both to eat its cake and have it. It desires the Divine Existence both to have that inescapable character which can, on modern views, only be found where truth reflects an arbitrary convention, and also the character of "making a real difference" which is only possible where truth doesn't have this merely linguistic basis.
> ... Modern views make it self-evidently absurd (if they don't make it ungrammatical) to speak of such a Being (i.e., one whose existence and attributes are inescapable and necessary) and attribute existence to him.[14]

His argument here is that the ontological argument does not leave the matter of divine existence inconclusive, as Kant would have it. Rather, it forces us to come down on the atheistic side!

Most of the replies to Findlay have been directed toward attacking some aspect of the modern assumption of the incompatibility of "necessity" and "existence." This sort of reply constitutes part of Norman Malcolm's excellent defense of Anselm's argument.[15] Another treatment of the matter works at undermining Findlay's central contention, namely, what it takes for God to be religiously adequate. This approach is worked out by Charles Hartshorne. We shall examine Malcolm's article first. In addition to attacking the incompatibility of "necessity" and "existence," it has the merit of setting Anselm's arguments before us in a clear and unmistakable fashion.

---

13. Ibid., 47.
14. Ibid., 54–55.
15. Malcolm, "Anselm's Ontological Arguments" in Plantinga, ed., *The Ontological Argument*, 136–80.

THREE TREATMENTS OF THE ONTOLOGICAL ARGUMENT

Malcolm

Malcolm is one of the very few persons to have noticed that Anselm actually presents *two quite different pieces of reasoning*. The first argument, that of the second chapter of *Proslogion*, is based on the premise that it is greater or more perfect to exist in reality than merely to exist in the understanding.[16] Malcolm, following Kant, shows that Anselm's reasoning here is fallacious, because it is based on "the false doctrine that existence is a perfection (and therefore that 'existence' is a 'real predicate')."[17] The doctrine is false because it is senseless.

However, the second argument, that of chapter 3 of *Proslogion*, does not depend on the false assumption that it makes sense to say that existence in reality is greater than existence merely in the understanding. It sets forth the quite different concept that "a being whose *nonexistence is logically impossible* is 'greater' than a being whose *nonexistence is logically possible* (and therefore that a being a greater than which cannot be conceived must be one whose nonexistence is logically impossible)."[18] Anselm's argument is as follows:

> It is possible to conceive of a being which cannot be conceived not to exist; and this is greater than one which can be conceived not to exist. Hence, if that than which nothing greater can be conceived, can be conceived not to exist, it is not that than which nothing greater can be conceived. But this is an irreconcilable contradiction. There is, then, so truly a being than which nothing greater can be conceived to exist, that it cannot be conceived not to exist; and this being thou art, O Lord, Our God.[19]

There are two things to notice about this form of the argument. First, Anselm continues to define God as perfection, or "that than which nothing greater can be conceived to exist." But this concept of perfection is not based on existence in reality as opposed to that in thought. It is a different category than that which might be the greatest of its kind. Thus the statement "Jones is the tallest man in the world" expresses an assertion about a fact that may be empirically checked. But that which is said to be such that nothing of *any* kind can even be conceived to be greater is of a wholly

---

16. Anselm, *St. Anselm* (trans. Deane), 7–8.
17. Malcolm, "Anselm's Ontological Arguments," 140.
18. Ibid., 141.
19. Anselm, *St. Anselm*, 8–9.

different order of being. Malcolm notes that perfection, as defined by Anselm, "expresses a logically necessary truth and not a mere matter of fact" such as that concerning Jones.[20]

The second thing to notice is that Anselm is saying that "a being which cannot be conceived not to exist" (one whose nonexistence is logically *impossible*) is greater than a being "which can be conceived not to exist" (one whose nonexistence is logically *possible*). Moreover, Anselm equates perfection with necessary existence. Malcolm states the principle of the second argument clearly:

> Previously I rejected *existence* as a perfection. Anselm is maintaining (in chapter three), not that existence is a perfection, but that *the logical impossibility of non-existence is a perfection*. In other words, necessary existence is a perfection. His first ontological proof uses the principle that a thing is greater if it exists than if it does not exist. His second proof employs the different principle that a thing is greater if it necessarily exists than if it does not necessarily exist.[21]

The distinction appears obvious—not "existence" but "necessary existence" is a perfection. Yet it is precisely this distinction so many critics of Anselm fail to make.

Malcolm attempts to make the concept of "necessary existence" intelligible by working out the consequences of contingency or dependence, and contrasting these with what must be the case for necessity. The result, as he notes, is similar to that of Findlay. Thus he says that the being about whom the Nicene Creed speaks cannot depend on anything for its existence; it is conceived "as an absolutely unlimited being."[22] Also, the concept includes *eternity* so that all duration is excluded from God's being.[23] Finally, necessary existence includes properties such as *necessary* omniscience and *necessary* omnipotence. This means that "omniscience" and "omnipotence" are "internal properties of the concept" of God and as such not subject to empirical testing. Therefore, Malcolm argues: "*Necessary existence* is a property of God in the *same sense* that *necessary omnipotence* and *necessary omniscience* are His properties. And we are not to think that 'God

---

20. Malcolm, "Anselm's Ontological Arguments," 142.
21. Ibid.
22. Ibid., 144.
23. Ibid., 144–45.

THREE TREATMENTS OF THE ONTOLOGICAL ARGUMENT

necessarily exists' means that it follows necessarily from something that God exists contingently."[24]

Put this way, the statement casts a light on Anselm's real discovery, namely, that God's existence is of such an order that it is a matter of *logical* necessity. The truth of the proposition "God exists" is in no way derived from, or refuted by, facts of contingent actuality. Consequently, Malcolm sees that the proposition "God exists" must be understood as an a priori proposition equivalent to "God necessarily exists." "In this sense," he writes, "Anselm's proof is a proof of God's existence."[25] In other words there really can be no cogent proof of God's existence *from empirical evidence* as St. Thomas would have us believe. On the other hand, neither can there be can a cogent *disproof* of God's existence *from empirical evidence* as several writers have alleged.[26] Either God's existence is logically necessary or logically impossible. Findlay, of course, saw this. And his argument was that the attempt to attach factual existence, or "the character of 'making a real difference'" to logically necessary existence vitiates it, making the concept logically impossible.

Perhaps Findlay was wrong in claiming that Anselm attempted "to build bridges between mere abstractions and concrete existence."[27] Malcolm has shown that the proposition "God exists" is an a priori proposition and, therefore, makes no claim to *factual* significance. But if this is all that can be said, has he not won a Pyrrhic victory? Even if the argument does not "build bridges" between the necessary and the contingent (the abstract and concrete existence), it is clear that theism does require that effort. The claim of theism is that God *does* make a difference in the world and in the affairs of men.

Still, Malcolm believes that more can be said. He challenges the commonly held assumption that "all existential propositions are contingent" by finding certain non-contingent propositions that seem clearly to assert the existence of something. For example, in Euclidean theory the theorem "there exists an infinite number of prime numbers" is an "existential proposition." Thus Malcolm asks: "Do we not want to say that *in some sense* it

---

24. Ibid., 147.
25. Ibid., 147.
26. E.g., J. L. Mackie, "Evil and Omnipotence," from *Mind*, reprinted in Pike, ed., *God and Evil*, 46–60; Flew, "Theology and Falsification," in *New Essays in Philosophical Theology*, 96–99.
27. Findlay, "Can God's Existence Be Disproved?," 47.

asserts the existence of something? Cannot we say, with equal justification, that the proposition 'God necessarily exists' asserts the existence of something *in some sense*?"[28] His point is that there are many senses in which propositions are used and that their differences are reflected in how they are supported: "There are as many kinds of existential propositions as there are subjects of discourse."[29]

In reply, it may reasonably be asked: In what sense does the proposition "God necessarily exists" assert something? We have seen that the way this assertion is supported is with logic and not facts! Perhaps it asserts the existence of some *special* language-game. Oddly enough, it is just this line of thought Malcolm finds persuasive. In commenting on a verse of Psalm 90, which ascribes eternity and, by implication, aseity to God, he writes:

> Here is expressed the idea of the necessary existence and eternity of God, an idea that is essential to the Jewish and Christian religions. In those complex systems of thought, those "language-games," God has the status of a necessary being. Who can doubt that? Here we must say with Wittgenstein, "This language-game is played!" I believe we may rightly take the existence of those religious systems of thought in which God figures as a necessary being to be a disproof of the dogma, affirmed by Hume and others, that no existential propositions can be necessary.[30]

The simplicity of this defense is impressive, but it only serves to delay the attack. One may readily admit that the idea of a necessary being is essential to certain complex systems of thought and still inquire whether the being, as *necessarily existent*, makes any difference in the lives of those who play this language-game. All sorts of factors in the system may affect them, but is not the necessary being, *as necessary*, compatible with anything at all happening? Another thorny question is: "Does not this view of religious language exclude itself from the canons of normal criticism?" Thus, it is not at all clear from Malcolm's claim that God, as necessarily existent, either makes any difference at all in the contingent world or can be rationally supported.

Moreover, when we unpack the notion of necessary existence, as Malcolm has been using it, we find incompatibilities within it. For example, in expanding the notion of perfection, he has shown that it must entail

---

28. Malcolm, "Anselm's Ontological Arguments," 149.
29. Ibid., 150.
30. Ibid., 153.

THREE TREATMENTS OF THE ONTOLOGICAL ARGUMENT

"eternity." But this notion excludes "as senseless all sentences that imply that it has duration." Yet he also finds that necessary omniscience is a requirement of the concept. But surely omniscience, even *necessary* omniscience, is knowledge of *all* reality—contingent and temporal facts as well as timeless truths. Clearly, to have knowledge of temporal events, of things which are passing, is to know them in the act of passage or from within. It is, in fact, to be involved in duration. Hence, eternity and omniscience, both of which are said to be internal requirements of the concept "necessary existence" are logically incompatible. Something is very wrong.

We may summarize the major points made so far:

1. Modern philosophical analysis has argued strongly that propositions are either necessary or existential or they are senseless;
2. Findlay has argued that a religiously adequate concept of God must be in all ways necessary, and that
3. on the basis of the modern view, to speak of such a God while attributing existence to him is self-evidently absurd;
4. Malcolm has shown that a careful analysis of the *second* form of the ontological argument reveals the logical equivalence of perfection and necessity;
5. He makes the additional claim that the proposition "God necessarily exists," asserts the existence of something in some sense, although God is in no way contingent.
6. We have argued that even though Malcolm's claim for the second form of the ontological argument is correct, and that it shows "necessary existence" to be of a different order from "contingent existence," he has not given sufficient grounds for showing that God "makes a real difference" in the contingent world. Moreover, we have given some reason to believe that the properties that are said to be inherent in a necessary being are, in some cases, incompatible with one another.

Now let us turn our attention to a reconsideration of what constitutes a religiously adequate object. In doing so we shall attempt to understand "necessity" such that a perfect being may be said to "*exist necessarily*," but

Hartshorne

Like both Findlay and Malcolm, Hartshorne is concerned with developing as clearly and fully as possible the concept of God while remaining faithful to the religious attitude. His idea of the "religious idea of perfection" is not, initially, unlike Findlay's. Hartshorne defines God as the being who "can be worshipped without incongruity by every individual no matter how exalted."[31] Plainly, this is akin to Findlay's understanding of the object adequate to the religious attitude, to which, he says, we wholly defer, abasing ourselves "with unquestioning enthusiasm." But this is where the similarity ceases. A comparison of their ideas of worship discloses much about the corresponding ideas of God.

We have shown that for Findlay worship means self-abasement, total deference, and unquestioning enthusiasm. This attitude, he believes, involves the worshipper in a feeling of "comparative nothingness." Moreover, this view of worship presumes an infinite gulf between the worshipper and his object such that the worshipper is incapable of participating in the excellences of the object. In this view, then, worship is a merely subjective exercise, affirming that the worshipper is inconsequential so far as the object is concerned. It neither allows for participation in the excellences of deity nor does it affect God in any way.

For Hartshorne the matter is quite otherwise. In worship we are enhanced, while at the same time we add to the actuality of God's life. "To worship X," he notes following the great commandment, "is to 'love' X with all one's heart and all one's mind and all one's soul and all one's strength." This means, he adds, that our entire life "is to have God as its object."[32] And the second great commandment is an inherent corollary: the love of neighbor and of self.

The first thing we should notice about this formula is that love, rather than self-abasement, is its key notion. For Hartshorne love is neither a passive, self-effacing relationship nor an aggressive, reward-seeking one. It is a relationship of mutual service and value-enhancement. In this relationship both the lover and the beloved are enriched. Love seeks neither for rewards

---

31. Hartshorne, *The Logic of Perfection*, 40.
32. Ibid., 40.

THREE TREATMENTS OF THE ONTOLOGICAL ARGUMENT

nor to escape punishment, but to contribute to the good that transcends the momentary individual, be that my enduring self, another self, a group, or God, who is the inclusive individual. Secondly, we should notice that the idea entails that worship is not an exclusively "religious" act separate from our secular lives, but that all one's life should be a "reasonable, holy and living sacrifice" to God.[33] Worship may well focus in liturgical acts, but essentially to love God fully means, at the very least, to love myself and my neighbors.

Worship, thus understood, is expansive even though it involves sacrifice. For sacrifice, unlike sheer loss, means suffering *for* someone or some cause with whom the fulfillment of my "real" self is bound up. And the ultimate "someone" or "cause" to whom we contribute and for whom we sacrifice is God, who is inclusive of all things. Hartshorne acknowledges that a person is demeaned if he merely serves a group that is not an individual and so cannot know or respond to him. But if, by promoting the good of the group (which means serving the needs of the individuals who compose it) he is serving God, the inclusive individual who knows all and responds to all, he is *not* demeaned.[34]

Now, a question arises concerning the adequacy of this concept of worship: Does it cover the full range of attitudes generally associated with worship, including the sense of contrition for sin? Without entering into the question of Hartshorne's sensitivity to the depth of sin in the human spirit,[35] we should observe that his thesis shares a conviction with many great spiritual counselors of the past and with many noted psychologists of the present, namely, that one's conscience is stimulated more fully and more healthfully in a mature love relationship than in a state of self-effacement.[36] In a mature form of love a person is open to the possibility of his having been wrong and knows quite well the sense of judgment that accompanies his harmful acts. A sense of contrition is by no means excluded from the view of worship that has love at its center. It seems, in fact, that Hartshorne's concept of worship is *more* adequate to the wide range of attitudes involved in traditional worship than is Findlay's. Findlay's understanding of the re-

---

33. *Book of Common Prayer*, cited in ibid., 257.

34. Hartshorne, *The Logic of Perfection*, 146.

35. See, for example, ibid., 318–23; and also, Hartshorne, *Reality as Social Process*, chapter 8.

36. E.g., Fromm, *Man for Himself*, 162–75; also Allport, *The Individual and His Religion*, 90–111.

ligious attitude may be one source of error in delineating what the object adequate to that attitude must be.

Let us now compare the corresponding concepts of God. Findlay says the object adequate to the religious attitude must have the following characteristics: (a) "superiority"; (b) "unsurpassable supremacy" in all respects; (c) infinitude; (d) unlimitedness; (e) "all-comprehensiveness" as the absolute source of all actual and possible beings and values; (f) necessary existence; (g) possession of its qualities in "some necessary manner."

This list lays bare what is included in the concept of perfection as it was classically understood. Perfection is, in Anselm's phrase, "that than which nothing greater can be conceived." And for Findlay, as well as for the tradition, this quite plainly entails being *in all ways complete*—(b), (d), (e)—and *necessary*—(f), (g). Hartshorne's claim is that this is precisely where we are required to make a fresh inquiry. The classical idea of perfection makes no distinction between the divine *individual* and divine *states*, or put another way, between the bare *existence* of perfection and its *actuality*. If we make this distinction, Hartshorne maintains, we find that having necessary existence does not require that all divine properties be necessary. How can this be? The remainder of the paper attempts to make this distinction clear and the idea of God that it entails cogent.

Anselm's definition of perfection is an excellent starting point, but it is not unambiguous. For "a being than which nothing greater can be conceived" may mean either: (1) that the being is such that no individual greater than God is conceivable, or (2) that not even God in a different state can be greater than God is now. The second meaning, accepted by Anselm and most of his critics as the sole possible meaning, does not consider alternative possible states of actuality as applicable to God. The first meaning does allow for this possibility and insists on the distinction between the divine individual and divine states. From the point of view of the first meaning we may conceive God as "the self-surpassing being that positively surpasses all others."[37] This definition means that, although it is inconceivable for another being to equal or surpass God, his current actual state is not the greatest possible state. Obviously, this concept of perfection entails that there is change in God. Classically, it was thought that to attribute change, suffering, dependency—any sort of relativity or contingency—to God was to attribute defect to him. In order to be perfect, so it went, God

---

37. Hartshorne, *Reality as Social Process*, 112.

must be absolute, unchanging, impassible, etc. In short, he must be in all ways complete.

Hartshorne forces us to take another look. If we consider the human analogy may we not learn something more about change and relativity? Do we not consider that to love is better or more perfect than not to love? And to love is, in part at least, to share another's joys and sorrows, to sympathize with him, to affect and be affected by him. As Rollo May says, "Hate is not the opposite of love; apathy is. The opposite of will is not indecision . . . but being uninvolved, detached, unrelated to the significant events . . . The interrelation of love and will inheres in the fact that both terms describe a person in the process of reaching out, moving towards the world, seeking to affect others or the inanimate world, and opening himself to be affected."[38] In short, to love involves change.

As helpful as understanding love, is the consideration of the ethical aspects. While it is acknowledged that moral instability is a defect, so too is rigidity or "dogmatism." To be sure, a moral and loving person will be steadfast in his active concern for the good of his fellow creatures, but that steadfastness does not rule out response to changing circumstances. Perhaps the early thinkers saw only the liabilities in change and relativity and not the positive aspects. Concerning the human analogue of perfection, Hartshorne writes: "A 'good' man is not, compared to a bad or inferior one, any less relative or contingent; but rather, he is more adequately related to other things and richer and more harmonious in his accidental qualities."[39] He remarks that inferior forms of relativity are to be found in our being too dependent upon *one* factor in the total environment, or else in being too sensitive to a *particular* aspect of the entire process. Yet, as he also notes, these deficiencies are not overcome by withdrawing into independence and insensitivity; the wise and good person responds to the needs of the moment, but he measures his response, taking into account the wider claims of the present, the past, and the future: "Balanced appropriateness in one's relativity to other things or persons, not non-relativity, is the mark of wisdom and goodness. The non-relative or merely inflexible person . . . need not be especially admired."[40]

The critic may ask if this is not precisely where the human analogy fails. Human goodness, wisdom, and love are related to the human mode

---

38. May, *Love and Will*, 29.
39. Hartshorne, *The Logic of Perfection*, 135.
40. Ibid., 135.

of existence proportionally to the relation of God's goodness, wisdom, and love to his mode of existence. But God's mode of existence is absolute and unchanging!

The radical distinction between the human and the divine modes of existence is not lost on Hartshorne. On the contrary he is persistent in demanding that we be aware of the difference between that unique, necessary mode of existence that is God's alone, and the contingent existence of all non-divine beings. But as it stands, this distinction does not reveal anything about the inadequacy of the analogy. For the distinction concerns mere existence abstracted from the concrete actuality of the beings under consideration. To see what is important about it let us look again at our case. We have looked at love, wisdom, and goodness, either divine or human. The important difference is that the human forms of these, at their very best, are restricted and so incapable of full flexibility. The divine form is unrestricted or infinitely flexible. Yet we see that in both cases we have genuine love, wisdom, and goodness—forms that are appropriate to their respective modes of existence. Thus Hartshorne writes: "What is eternally fixed or absolute in God is exactly the unlimited flexibility of His capacity to know and value, and thus to relativize Himself. He is immutably capable, to an ideal degree and in an ideal manner, of self-enrichment through anything that may become real."[41] To insist that God's love, wisdom, and goodness are absolute and unchanging, therefore, means that God is steadfastly loving, wise, and good with respect to all beings. However, to insist that the actual content of God's being remains unchanged as he steadfastly knows, values, and loves the changing content of the world is to deny that he knows or loves the world in any meaningful sense.

Now, as the result of these reflections on the mutability of individuals with respect to loving, knowing, and valuing, we may grasp the importance of comparing individuals, not only with other individuals, but with earlier states of themselves. When we consider the relation of "superiority," we must consider the reflexive case—superiority or inferiority to past states of myself—as well as the cases of relation to other individuals. For example, we may say that a person, at twenty-five, has a richer life, and is, therefore, "superior" to himself at the age of three months. Likewise, we may say that the same person late in life, having physically deteriorated, is "inferior" to himself with respect to his former state of maturity. Interestingly, and importantly, the only instances in which no change can be found,

---

41. Ibid., 101.

THREE TREATMENTS OF THE ONTOLOGICAL ARGUMENT

where self-superiority or self-inferiority are inapplicable, are the instances of qualities as abstracted from the concrete individual. Thus Hartshorne writes: "An abstraction as such obviously cannot grow or decline, but is fixed regardless of what happens. Only the concrete can be more or less, while still being itself. Self-identity in growth or decay is the mark of real individuals. Abstract qualities abstract from, omit, precisely the living process of growth from quality to quality . . . Self-surpassing is characteristic, not . . . of the imperfect versus the perfect but of the concrete and individual versus the abstract and merely universal."[42]

On the basis of this insight we can recognize that to worship the absolute and unchanging is to worship an abstraction and not the perfect individual as such. Indeed, by moving from the general case of *any* individual as concrete and changing, but having qualities that are abstract and constant, to the particular case of the *perfect* individual, we may understand "perfection" in two senses: on the one hand, perfection taken as an absolute must be an abstract quality (particularly the quality of necessarily existing); on the other hand, the reflexive sense (surpassing self as well as others) of perfection is the perfection of a concrete individual, and concrete individuals must be relative. To be sure, the perfect individual, God, is not merely relative in the ordinary sense, which entails the notion of finitude or contingency of existence. The relativity attaching to perfection is thus the unique case of the "superrelative," which is an all-inclusive concept.[43] The perfect individual is inclusive of abstract factors, such as that it necessarily exists and must be somehow actualized, that it steadfastly loves, knows, and values all beings, but is also inclusive of the lives of all other individuals that come into being. Superrelative perfection is, therefore, contingent upon all other individuals for the content of its life, which is enriched by their lives.

But why should we assume that the perfect individual can only increase, when it is apparent that all other individuals both increase and decrease with respect to former states? A small amount of reflection gives us the answer. The perfect individual is related to everything. He, preeminently, knows and loves all beings. And he is, on the principles by which we have operated, infinitely flexible in valuing everything that comes into existence. As we noted, God "is immutably capable to an ideal degree and in an ideal manner, of self-enrichment through anything that may become real." You and I may decrease, but our lives will have added to the sum total

42. Ibid., 114.
43. Ibid., 122–23.

of all that has been. Thus the only way for the perfect individual, who is inclusive of all that has been, not to surpass former states of himself would be for the whole of finite reality to come to a standstill or cease.[44]

Now we may return to the ontological argument and see the difference this concept of perfection as "the self-surpassing being that positively surpasses all others" can make. We saw that Anselm, in the last line of his second argument, equated perfection with necessary existence. This seemed both required and desirable. But it, also, has shown itself to involve incompatibilities on the assumption that necessary existence entails complete necessity. The demand for the necessity of the perfect being, combined with the requirement that it have the character of "making a real difference" in the contingent world, renders it absurd or impossible.

However, if we conceive perfection in the way that we have argued that religion demands, the dilemma fades away. For on the religiously influenced conception, God is the supremely concrete individual who is related to all the world and whose necessary existence is the common factor abstracted from the full actuality of his changing, and in some ways, contingent life! Here, then, we are enabled to say, "perfection necessarily exists" with logical consistency, without demanding of the perfect *individual* some of the absurdities that are wrongly thought to be corollaries of necessary existence.

This argument, perhaps, becomes more cogent the clearer we are as to what necessity means with respect to God. We remember the general consensus among modern philosophers that necessity refers to what is *logically* true, or true simply by virtue of the terms employed; it is true under any condition whatever. Thus no contingent facts are relevant to necessity. Although many philosophers assume that necessity has only to do with propositions, Hartshorne (and surely Findlay and Malcolm) believes that the concept is equally applicable to propositions and to the wider range of reality, and he gives reasons for this belief. In the second sense, necessity is the abstract residuum which is common to all things, or, "what all possible

---

44. It is doubtful that the Law of Entropy or increasing disorder, which applies to a *closed system*, is applicable to the universe as a whole. In any case, the ultimate intuition upon which Hartshorne's whole philosophy is reared is that the universe is *not* closed, but is *creative*. Thus he writes: "Reality as a whole of real events, together with whatever there may be beside events, is a growing whole. . . . It is mutable but incorruptible." *Reality as Social Process*, 119. Cf. also his arguments in *Creative Synthesis and Philosophic Method*, chaps. 1, 9, and 10.

states of reality have in common."[45] It is what the tradition has meant by "being itself."

Now, with respect to the perfect individual, necessity means the bare necessity to exist in some state or other. Had Anselm been free of his Greek philosophical bias, Hartshorne thinks, he would have seen that "God's necessary existence must be very different indeed from His total concrete or factual reality. The divine necessity is *that* such abstract traits or 'perfections' 'as knowing all there is to know' must be realized in some form, with respect to some concrete world of knowable things, but not necessarily in the form and with respect to the world which actually obtain."[46] The full force of his conviction is made in the following passage:

> God *merely* as necessary is less than any contingent thing whatever, even the meanest. To worship the necessary is but a subtle form of idolatry... For God as necessary is God considered under an extreme abstraction, God as barely existing somehow, in some state of concrete actuality or other, no matter what. But God cannot be limited to His merely necessary being; He is the individual that could not fail to be actualized in some contingent particular form. This implies an immeasurable superiority; but what actualized the superiority is God-now, or God-then, not just God at any time or as eternal, which is a mere abstraction. The necessity that there be some contingent actuality is inherent in the unique abstractness of the identifying divine individuality or essence.[47]

On this understanding of the abstractness of necessity and of the concreteness of the perfect individual who *necessarily* actualizes himself in some state or other—*and only on this understanding*—can we avoid the dilemma Findlay showed to inhere in the ontological argument as applying to the idea of God as in all ways necessary. God's necessity as such does not, and cannot, make "a real difference." *That* perfection exists necessarily—a mode totally other than contingent existence—is logically true, but abstract. *What* the content of perfection is, is contingent upon what actually becomes, and in turn makes a "real difference" in the contingent world.

In summary let us note the following points: Malcolm shows clearly that Anselm's major proof concerns the perfection of *necessary existence*, not mere existence. Findlay, having seen this, thinks, on the basis of what

---

45. Hartshorne, *Anselm's Discovery*, 43.
46. Ibid., 48.
47. Hartshorne, *The Logic of Perfection*, 102.

he takes to be the demands of religious adequacy, that it entails total necessity, which, when combined with the character of being factually significant, is absurd. Hence, he concludes that necessary existence is impossible. Hartshorne, agreeing that the proof concerns necessary existence, argues strongly that this is an abstract feature belonging to the perfect individual. But, on the basis of what *he* takes to be the demands of religious adequacy, the perfect individual must be concrete and "superrelative" and so factually significant. The two "perfections" can be combined because the abstract is contained within the concrete.

8

IDEAS AND IMAGES OF GOD

A TALK FOR THE PASADENA VILLAGE

David R. Mason
2013

There are a great many reasons that thoughtful and sensitive people in today's world are skeptical about God and religious claims or else are plainly atheistic. I suspect, however, that most of the reasons fall into two categories: (1) the "God" in question is one who is utterly *immoral*, repugnant to our basic sense of decency; (2) the religious claims associated with this God are *incredible*, flying in the face of commonsense, the findings of science, and principles of sound reason. To illustrate these one could cite many biblical passages that speak of God as a distant patriarch, or a king slaughtering thousands of persons. Then there are the many passages that have God playing favorites, or passages that make incredible claims (e.g., the many "miracles" that ignore or flout the laws of nature, including virgin birth stories, bringing dead people back to life, and having people fly up into the air to be with God). The immorality and the senselessness of religious claims are sharply put by Sam Harris. Speaking of the issue of "theodicy"—how believers try to justify an omniscient, omnipotent, and benevolent God in the teeth of the recurrence of evils of the worst kind—Harris says:

"Somewhere in the world a man has abducted a little girl. Soon he will rape, torture, and kill her. If an atrocity of this kind is not occurring at precisely this moment, it will happen in a few hours, or days at most. Such is the confidence we can draw from the statistical laws that govern the lives of six billion human beings. The same statistics also suggest that this girl's parents believe—as you [Christians or religious people] believe—that an all-powerful and all-loving God is watching over them and their family. Are they right to believe this? Is it *good* that they believe this? No. *The entirety of atheism is contained in this response.*"[1]

On the other hand, Harris insists that believers "should be obliged to present evidence for [God's] existence—and indeed for His benevolence, given the relentless destruction of innocent human beings we witness in the world each day. An atheist is a person who believes that the murder of a single little girl—even once in a billion years—casts doubt upon the idea of a benevolent God." Moreover, he cites all sorts of examples from contemporary life, of "God's failure to protect humanity," but one such is the destruction of Hurricane Katrina: "More than a thousand people died" in New Orleans; "tens of thousands lost all their earthly possessions; and nearly a million were displaced." Most people in New Orleans shared a "belief in an omnipotent, omniscient, and compassionate God. But what was God doing while Katrina laid waste to their city? Surely He heard the prayers of those elderly men and women who fled the rising waters for the safety of their attics, only to be slowly drowned there ... These poor people died talking to an imaginary friend."

We should consider the age-old problem of theodicy as solved, Harris concludes: "If God exists, either He can do nothing to stop the most egregious calamities, or He does not care to. God, therefore, is either impotent or evil ... There is another possibility, of course, and it is both the most reasonable and least odious: the biblical God is a fiction, like Zeus and the thousands of other dead gods whom most sane human beings now ignore."[2]

I am bound to take the sensibility here expressed very seriously, for it lays bare what no reasonable or moral person could possibly accept. And, if this were all that believers had to cling to, we would be bound to be skeptics or, better, atheists. But I am also convinced that the idea of God presupposed here, by believer and atheist alike, is not the only option we have. It does not take account of several significant ideas and images of God that have emerged, along with science, respect for reason, and the moral sensitivity to equal rights in our day. Moreover, the "God" presupposed by the typical believer and atheist is inferior to the "God" represented by these more recent ideas and images taken together.

1. Harris, *Letter to a Christian Nation*, 50–51.
2. Harris, *Letter to a Christian Nation*, 51–56.

IDEAS AND IMAGES OF GOD

The newer ideas are:

1. God does *not know the future* as already determined;
2. God *changes* as God interacts with a changing world;
3. God's power is *not the power to coerce or manipulate*, but rather is the *power of love, the power of reasonable persuasion*;
4. God is *not* to be regarded as a *dominant male figure*, but God *is* properly understood as *personal*;
5. God is *not separate and distant from the world*, but God is *inclusive of the world*.

Let us inspect each idea singly, and then show that the "God" represented by these ideas and images taken together is intelligible, morally sound, and worthy of worship.

(1) "God does *not know the future* as already determined." For ages philosophers and theologians thought that for God to be "omniscient" meant that God must know all "past, present, and future" *at once*, which is to say, as already actual or determinate. For instance St. Thomas Aquinas, with his well-known simile of a being at a great height seeing all who travel a road "at once," says that, whereas we live successively, "God knows contingent things, not successively, as they are in their own being, as we do, but *simultaneously* . . . His *knowledge is measured by eternity*, as is His being, and *eternity, being simultaneously whole, comprises all time* . . . Hence, all things that are in time *are present to God from eternity.*" And Thomas insists: "Things reduced to actuality in time are known by us successively, in time, but by God they are known in eternity, which is above time. Whence to us they cannot be certain, since we know future contingent things only as contingent futures (i.e., *as possibilities*); but they are certain to God alone, whose understanding is in eternity above time."[3]

Here, *humans* and all creatures are rightly regarded as *temporal*, that is as living "successively." But *God* is taken to be *eternal*, that is, above and outside time altogether. So God, the omniscient being, by this way of reckoning, must know *everything* as present and "certain" or already actual and determinate, even though "future contingent things" are *not* certain to us who are temporal beings. For us they are not present, nor are they actual or determinate; they are but *possibilities*. But, if God knows what seem to us to be but mere possibilities *as actualities*, we are mistaken; they *are* actualities.

---

3. Aquinas, *Basic Writings of Saint Thomas Aquinas*, 155–56; my emphasis.

God cannot know falsely. Therefore, what God knows eternally already is. Moreover, Aquinas had made all this evident a few pages earlier where he insists that "the knowledge of God (that is, God's knowledge) is the *cause* of things... It is manifest that God causes things by His intellect, since His being is His act of understanding; and hence His knowledge must be the cause of things, in so far as His will is joined to it."[4] As many have said, "for God to foreknow is to foreordain."

This whole way of conceiving divine knowledge is, at best, problematic although it continues to dominate the usual way of thinking about God. In fact, it makes a mockery of the notion of "omniscience." But from the sixteenth century, at least, a growing cadre of progressive thinkers has argued that it makes no sense to think that an omniscient being could know the future as if it had already occurred. The Italian priest, Socinus (1539–1604), observed that what was "eternal" about God was simply that God "exists and cannot not exist," but that this does not mean that God's knowledge, and in fact God's life, should be simultaneous: "if it were correct that God knows the future as determinate, there would be nothing accidental or contingent... Everything must then be necessary and determined from all eternity, since from all eternity known by God. But then there is no human freedom. There is also [according to the hypothesis] no divine freedom, since from all eternity God could act only as he actually does act."[5] So Socinus concluded that God could only know the future as that which was *possible*, not what was already actual.

This understanding of God's knowledge developed through the next few centuries, especially by philosophers and theologians known as "process philosophers," and has recently been given currency by a group of Evangelical theologians called "open theists." They say that God knows everything that happened in the past and is happening now, but God has no foreknowledge of events because the future has not happened. Moreover, they see, as Socinus saw and as all process thinkers see, that if God actually did know the future as determined God would have determined the outcome of all things that happen in the world including all the bad things. This is what the atheists take to be the case. But, since God does not—and *cannot*—know the future as already determined, God is *not* responsible for particular ills in the world.

---

4. Aquinas, *Basic Writings of Saint Thomas Aquinas*, 147; my emphasis.
5. In Hartshorne and Reese, eds., *Philosophers Speak of God*, 225–26.

IDEAS AND IMAGES OF GOD

So, we can confidently assert that God is genuinely *omniscient* in the only way that makes sense; God knows all the past as actual and the present as it is coming to be; but God can only know the future as the realm of *possibilities*. God has an open future.

(2) "God *changes* as God interacts with a changing world." The insight that God has an open future, that God faces unactualized possibilities not all of which can be actualized, carries with it the realization that God changes as God interacts with a changing world and that God is affected by what we do and say. This should have been clear from the religious conviction that we make a difference to God when we pray and when we simply go about our lives in the world: God hears, sees, and is affected by what we do and God suffers with the suffering of the world. For example God says to Moses at the burning bush: "I have observed the misery of my people who are in Egypt; I have heard their cry on account of their task masters. Indeed, I know their sufferings, and I have come down to deliver them" (Exod 3:7–8). Or, in the New Testament, not only does Jesus say that when we pray God hears, is affected, and responds appropriately, but Christ on the cross cries out: "My God, my God, why have you forsaken me?" (Mark 15:34) And Christians sense that this means that God has not forsaken him, but that God suffers with Christ in his hour of suffering. So Bonhoeffer understands this from his prison cell and says, "Only the suffering God can help."[6] And Whitehead, deeply influenced by what he calls "the Galilean vision of humility," remarks: "God is the great companion—the fellow-sufferer who understands."[7] God is affected by our plight; our lives make a difference to God. God is changed by what we suffer and what we do.

But haven't believers relied upon the idea that God is *absolute* or *immutable*, and so is immune to suffering and change? True, we hear Isaiah say: "All people are grass, their constancy is like the flower of the field . . . The grass withers, the flower fades, *but the word of our God will stand forever*" (Isa 40:6, 8). And we sing: "Immortal, invisible God only wise . . . We blossom and flourish like leaves on the tree, then wither and perish, *but nought changeth thee.*"[8]

Yes, but theologians (and philosophers, and ordinary folks) have failed to see what it is about God that is constant or even "immutable," and what it must be about God—or any individual—that changes. We can properly say

---

6. Bonhoeffer, *Letters and Papers from Prison*, 361.

7. Whitehead, *Process and Reality*, 351.

8. *The Hymnal 1982*, # 423.

that the fact *that God exists and cannot fail to exist* is immutable or absolute. And we can also say that God consistently *wills* the best for individuals in their given situation (often the given situation is such that the best for that individual in that particular situation is not all that good); but we cannot say that God determines the outcome or that God is immune to change. And we can also say that God inevitably *loves unconditionally,* but this means that God always cares, loves, and suffers with each individual, that God feels the feelings of others; God is affected by what we do. Only this way can God redeem or makes as good as possible what can be redeemed. Even so, all this means that *the individual, God, changes, grows with every encounter.* So we can say that the God who always exists, who inevitably wills the best, loves all, and responds to all, the God who knows what can be known—this God *changes* in the content of God's life just as any person changes by virtue of interactions with others. Abstractions may remain the same; it can be said that they are immutable. Real persons, however, are affected, interact, change, grow; to be a person is to relate, to be social, to love, to grow, to change. God is supremely loving and social; God changes.

(3) "God's power is *not the power to coerce or manipulate* (unilateral power); but rather it is *the power of love, the power of reasonable persuasion* (relational power)." For ages believers and atheists alike have thought that "omnipotence" meant the power to intervene and manipulate and/or reverse situations, the power to break or suspend the natural law, to change the natural course of events and to eliminate causes that produce bad outcomes, to reshape persons, things, and events (for the benefit of special interest groups); in short, to perform miracles. This understanding of power is, I believe, neatly illustrated in a few lines of A. A. Milne's childhood poem: "If I Were King":

"I often wish I were a King, *And then I could do anything.*

"I think, if I were King of Greece, *I'd push things off the mantelpiece.*

"If I were King of Timbuctoo, I'd think of lovely things to do.

"If I were King of anything, I'd tell the soldiers, '*I'm the King!*'"[9]

This product of childish fantasy, I suspect, lies at the base of and informs much understanding of "omnipotence"—the power to intervene and rearrange events and things, to manipulate persons, and to reverse bad

---

9. Milne, *The World of Christopher Robin,* 111.

outcomes. And it is what lends credence to the argument of Sam Harris and others (Hume had said it two centuries ago) that an omniscient, omnipotent, and benevolent God would not allow all the ugly, evil things to occur—hence "there is no God."

To be sure, Aquinas had tried to salvage a workable understanding of omnipotence when he observed that "nothing that implies a contradiction falls under the scope of God's omnipotence."[10] In other words, omnipotence is not to be construed as the ability to do that which is logically impossible. But Aquinas and others failed to apply this insight to significant cases. For instance: knowing eternally and simultaneously *as actual* that which is not actual but only a *possibility*; or eliminating freedom from free beings by determining all outcomes; or abrogating the natural effects of past causes; or reversing time. Most of these are what we have thought of as morally offensive, but they are also logically contradictory, and so should not be seen as having to do with "supreme power."

But there are other ways of coming at real divine power and some are ancient even if neglected by the theological tradition. The first I want to mention is the "divine" power to bring about a real created order from "chaos" by "reasonable persuasion." This might be gotten from a certain way of reading the first chapter of Genesis or the prologue to the Gospel of John, but we find it clearly in Plato's creation myth in the *Timaeus*. There the "creator god" called the "Demiurge" working with what Plato calls the "errant cause" or what we might understand as chaos—but it is not sheer nothingness—creates or generates this orderly universe by "the victory of reasonable persuasion" over the errant cause.[11]

Commenting on this in the twentieth century Alfred North Whitehead says that a "first phase" in the history of religion "is constituted by Plato's publication of his final conviction . . . that the divine element in the world is to be conceived as a persuasive agency and not as a coercive agency. This doctrine should be looked upon as one of the greatest intellectual discoveries in the history of religion."

Whitehead continues:

> The second phase is the supreme moment in religious history, according to the Christian religion. The essence of Christianity is the appeal to the life of Christ as a revelation of the nature of God and of his agency in the world . . . There can be no doubt as to

---

10. Aquinas, *Basic Writings of Saint Thomas Aquinas*, 265.
11. Plato, *Plato's Cosmology: The Timaeus*, 160.

what elements in the record have evoked a response from all that is best in human nature. The Mother, the Child, the bare manger: the lowly man, homeless and self-forgetful, with his message of peace, love, and sympathy: the suffering, the agony, the tender words as life ebbed, the final despair: and the whole with the authority of supreme victory.

Can there be any doubt [Whitehead asks rhetorically] "that the power of Christianity lies in its revelation in *act* of that which Plato divined in theory?"[12]

Whitehead's comment might suggest that it is only in the New Testament, and not throughout the Bible, that supreme power as "the victory of reasonable persuasion" is affirmed. Indeed, Whitehead shared with many persons of his day the false view that the Old Testament God is simply a God of wrath or of coercive power whereas the New Testament God is the God of love. Yet the power of divine agency as "steadfast love" is attested everywhere in the Hebrew Scriptures. From the testimony of Exodus in which God speaks compassionately: "I have observed the misery of my people . . . I have heard their cry . . . I know their suffering, and I have come down to deliver them" to "the Lord God is merciful and gracious, slow to anger, and abounding in steadfast love and faithfulness" (Exod 34:6 and *passim*); to Hosea's God: "When Israel was a child, I loved him, out of Egypt I called my son . . . it was I who taught Ephraim to walk, I took them up in my arms, but they did not know that I healed them. I led them with cords of human kindness, with bands of love, I was to them like those who lift infants to their cheeks, I bent down to them and led them" (Hos 11:1, 3–4); to Micah's God who cries out: "Oh my people, what have I done to you? In what have I wearied you? Answer me. For I brought you up out of the land of Egypt, and redeemed you from the house of slavery . . . And what does the Lord require of you but to do justice, and to love kindness, and to walk humbly with your God" (Mic 6:3–4, 8). In fact, I think the defining characteristic of God in the Hebrew Scriptures is "steadfast love."

Even so, it is also true, as Whitehead's comment makes explicit, that the life and death of Jesus as the Christ are proclaimed as the decisive "revelation of the nature of God and of God's agency in the world." God's agency, i.e., God's power, is the power of compassionate or suffering love: God is "the great companion—the fellow-sufferer who understands." The Gospels everywhere bear witness to this, but it is neatly summed up in John

---

12. Whitehead, *Adventures of Ideas*, 214

IDEAS AND IMAGES OF GOD

3:16: "God so loved the world that he gave his only Son, so that everyone who believes in him may not perish but may have eternal life." And the First letter of John distills this even more. Here John says several times, "God is love" (1 John 4:8, 16) and this means that God is the source of all love because God is supremely loving: "We love because he first loved us" (1 John 4:19). God's power, therefore, is not the power to act unilaterally for our good, but the power of love, the inexhaustible compassion that understands all because it is affected by all and suffers with all; this is the power of reasonable persuasion.

(4) God is *not* to be regarded as a *dominant male* figure, but God *is* properly understood as *personal*." There can be little doubt that one of the most consistently employed images of God in the Bible and in subsequent Jewish, Christian, and Muslim literature is that of a powerful male figure whether as creator, patriarch, king, or even as father. Since the 1970s, however, increasing numbers of mainline Christian and reformed Jews, in their liturgies and translations of Scripture, have changed, dropped, or replaced the male image. Not only have they removed the male pronoun—*he, his, him*—when referring to God; they often change terms such as "Lord," "King" (and 'kingdom"), and even "Father," when speaking of God, and "Son of God" or "Son of Man" with respect to the Messiah or Christ. They often replace these terms with less masculine-seeming words such as simply "God," or "Creator," or "Spirit," or "the Chosen One."

I believe that the ancients were right to have perceived God as personal, but that fixing on the *image* of the personal deity as *a man* was wrong.

In a male-dominated culture, so clearly evident in the Bible, men held nearly all positions of power and leadership (patriarchs, pharaohs, chieftains, warriors, kings, generals, emperors, priests, etc.) whereas women were secondary figures with little power or ingenuity (there are a few notable exceptions in the Bible such as Miriam, Deborah and Jael, Ruth, Esther, Judith, Mary Magdalene, and Mary the mother of Jesus, but none of them rises to the level of an Abraham, Moses, David, a Jesus, or Paul). Men were held to be the procreators as well as the progenitors of the tribe. Women were typically regarded as at best help-mates, at worst mere objects. Therefore, it seemed natural and proper for the writers of Scripture (men?) to project the male image onto the most powerful being in their life, their liberator and their creator. And so, many believers equated God's being a person with God's being a male.

LECTURES AND ESSAYS

If the fundamental biblical intuition that God is a personal being, rather than a nonpersonal one such as an abstraction or a mere force, is correct, then our task becomes that of depicting the essentials of being persons that does not limit persons to the male gender. What can we say with assurance? If we sweep away the many culturally dependent elements that accrue to ideas we find that all persons anywhere and at any time must be: *social, temporal, complex-yet-centered individuals*, with *memory, will, creativity, the ability to think and to "know that they know," and the capacity to interact with their environment.*

In other words all persons are selves or souls who are intimately interactive with particular bodies and with a wider community of others; they are "individuals-in-community" even though a community itself is not a person. (Despite the majority opinion in the Supreme Court's "Citizens United" case, a group or a "corporation" is *not* a "person.") Persons *are* individuals, although they are not separate or isolated individuals; they are acted on and influenced by others and, in turn, they act on and influence others. They are temporal, having a past they can call to mind with varying degrees of success, and they decide in each present, and they can imagine future possibilities; they can remember, will, act, and hope. Persons can mentally survey the world about them (and within them), inspect differences, create patterns, give order to reality, criticize old mistakes; they can think. Moreover, persons can be conscious that they and the world exist; they can know that they are and that they know (computers cannot be "persons").

The greatest expression of personhood, I believe, is "love." Human love entails mutuality or reciprocity, the ability and willingness to be acted on by others, together with the desire to respond in ways that optimize others' power, freedom, and richness of life. As Erich Fromm pointed out years ago, mature love entails concern for the well-being of the other, respect for the integrity of the other, responsibility or the ability to respond to the needs of the other, and intimate knowledge of the other together with the intense desire for the other's growth.[13] Love has nothing to do with gender, nor is it "power over" the other, the unilateral, coercive kind of power typically associated with male dominance. But, as we have seen, the power of love, "steadfast love," that inexhaustible compassion that understands all because it is affected by all and suffers with all is the most lasting and genuine power.

---

13. Fromm, *The Art of Loving*, 23–27.

IDEAS AND IMAGES OF GOD

God is not to be regarded as male, but God is loving, and so personal, in the supreme degree.

(5) "God is *not separate and distant from the world*, but God *is inclusive of the world*." I think it is safe to say that, for the most part, in our theistic tradition (i.e., Judaism, Christianity, and Islam), God has been regarded as separate from the world, over against it, even above the world. Insofar as God was thought to act in the world God would "come down" and intervene from without. Divine "transcendence" seen in spatial terms—God *above* the world—was understood such that God could never be intimately connected with the world.

There was a minority report, however, that survived for centuries out of sight of the theologians, but did not emerge as a legitimate idea of God until the twentieth century. In the Acts of the Apostles Paul is depicted as speaking to the Athenians who, he says, are "extremely religious in every way" particularly because they had an altar set up to "an unknown god" that they were searching for. And this god, Paul says, is "not far from each of us," for "in him we live and move and have our being" (Acts 17: 22, 23, 28). This intuition, that we live and move and have our being *in* God, probably borrowed from the Stoics, has been reshaped and developed in the modern world into a legitimate theological viewpoint called "panentheism."

Pan*en*theism (all things are *in* God), *not* to be confused with *pantheism*, regards God and the world as interrelated with the world being *in* God and yet God being *in* the world. This offers a viable alternative to both traditional theism and pantheism. Traditional theism typically *separated* God from the world only to have God intervene in the world abolishing all freedom and suspending all natural law or else simply to have God determine everything from eternity, thus nullifying time. Traditional pantheism *identified* God and the world and so retained sheer divine determinism without the need for outside intervention. Also, it eliminated creaturely individuality and freedom and, because the whole was understood to be static or unchanging, was utterly devoid of any real temporality.

Panentheism conceives God as the supreme inclusive whole interactive with its parts. Unlike pantheism the whole is temporal and ongoing, for there are continuously new possibilities to be enacted. The whole is conceived as a *personal whole* that continuously opens up new horizons for the cells of its body that themselves are continuously being born anew; thus the whole lures or persuades the parts to enact ideal possibilities. The parts, in turn, make their choices about what to enact (always within the limitations of their given situations). By deciding for themselves they thereby act in the ensuing world and also into the ongoing whole: "We live and move and have our being *in* God."

The best image for picturing this whole-part interaction, as I have already suggested, is the "mind-brain" or the "soul-body" image. Here the mind or the soul is the personal whole; the cells constitutive of the brain or the body are the parts that make up the body or the world.

We can, today, make sense of the interpenetration of the body and the soul, the physical and the mental, or, as we sometimes say, the interaction of all component parts of the psycho-physical organism. If we think of the soul or psyche as inclusive of the body we have an adequate model for understanding the personal God of the Bible. If we understand the soul as active in the bodily cells, even as the component parts of the physical organism affect the state of the soul, we have a way of understanding God's interactivity with the parts that make up the world without lapsing into a false and morally repugnant misconception of divine power as omnipotence.

* * * *

I believe that if we take all five of these ideas together we have the portrait of a God who is morally attractive and, at the same time, credible to thoughtful persons. Clearly, this God is omniscient in the only intelligible way a being could be: God knows all past and present as determinate, but the future only as what it is, namely, as the realm of possibilities; God, like all individuals has an open future. Therefore, God changes as God interacts with a changing, temporal world. This means that God is affected by what happens in the world, by what we decide, what we do. In turn, this insight shows that God's "power" should never have been thought of as unilateral power that determines the outcome of everything or even as the power to intervene miraculously in the world running roughshod over natural causation and finite freedom. Rather it is the supreme relational power, the power of reasonable persuasion and the power of love. Thus God is rightly regarded as personal, but should not be symbolized as male. God's role as agent in the world is to offer to creatures the best possibilities, given the constraints of their actual situation, for them to freely enact. As such God is the ground both of freedom and order in the world. And, as we have seen, this God is best symbolized as the personal whole in whom all the parts live and move and have their being, the soul or mind interacting with the neurons of the brain and, by extension, the cells of its body. The world in its complexity is the "body of God." God is the "World Soul" that is *in* all, and yet encompasses all, embracing them everlastingly in God's ongoing life.

9

THE LAST THINGS

A CHRISTIAN DOCTRINE OF HOPE

(David R. Mason, *Something That Matters:
A Theology for Critical Believers*.
Santa Barbara, CA: Praeger, 2011,
Chapter 10, pp. 140–58)

Because hope must inevitably be grounded in faith, the doctrine of the "last things" is really but an elaboration of our first principle, namely, that we live as humans at all only in the abiding confidence that we, and all creatures, are finally "something that matters." The Christian faith, which may be said to be a sharper, more explicit form of this common faith of humanity, holds that all creatures make a difference not only to our fellow beings which constitute our finite environment but to God revealed by Jesus Christ as the Father whose pure unbounded love redeems "all creatures great and small." God is the all-inclusive One "unto whom all hearts are open, all desires known, and from whom no secrets are hid." Thus the Christian hope is in the love of God that redeems and makes of everlasting value all finite acts and experiences. Nothing that occurs is either ignored or swept away; it is treasured for what it is and can be, and is saved for evermore in the ongoing life of God. In God alone there is no lapse of memory and nothing is lost or misinterpreted; in God alone the full ramifications of all deeds are felt and fully appreciated. Only in the life of God can any experience or occasion be valued adequately and with full understanding, full compassion. Only as

THE LAST THINGS

it is "objectively immortal"¹ in God can any occasion, finally, be said to be "something that matters."

Objections to this Expression of the Doctrine of Hope

No sooner, however, does a person thus summarily state the basis for and meaning of Christian hope than he or she can expect to hear objections raised from two opposing sides: from the side of traditional religion comes the objection that such talk of "objective immortality" appears as but a desiccated version of the hope for a resurrected life in which the faithful live immortal lives in full, conscious relationship with God, which is the real hope of any full-blooded believer. All talk of "objective immortality," so the objection goes, implies that we are to be nothing more than a "pulse in the Eternal mind,"² and surely we hope for more than that.

From the other side—that of the secular critics of religion—comes the objection that all such talk is but a desperate attempt to avoid "hostile life." Is not that hope of immortality but an "illusion"? And does it not act as the "*opium* of the people" that numbs the pain of the real world even as it turns us toward that "illusory sun"?³

We should keep these objections in mind, and sooner or later address them, as we endeavor to work out an adequate and intelligible eschatology. Meanwhile, let us begin with aspects of "hostile life" that Christian and biblical religion knows all too well and always endeavors to respond to pastorally:

Questions Raised from the Experience of Life

One of the most insistent and challenging—not to say, troubling—questions that forces itself upon any of us at one time or another is, "What is the

---

1. The phrase is Whitehead's and it stands for the doctrine that every actuality or occasion of experience, as it attains determinate status in the temporal world, becomes significant beyond itself, and finally is registered everlastingly and attains "unfading importance" in the life of God. See *Process and Reality*, xiii–xiv, 45, 351, and throughout the text.

2. Brooke, "The Soldier," 1827.

3. The critical phrases are the well-known ones of Freud and Marx. See Freud, *The Future of an Illusion*, 38–71, especially 63; and Marx, "Toward a Critique of Hegel's Philosophy of Right," in *Basic Writings*, 263.

meaning of life?" or, in reflecting on humdrum or tragic experience, "Is this *all* that life has to offer?" And, of course, implied by these questions is the even more haunting question, "What is the meaning of death—of my own death in particular?"

It is true, of course, that life has been kind to many of us who have been born in good health and into comfortable social and economic conditions that reward productivity so that we experience what we do, and what is done to us, as of real value. Even so, we, upon whom fortune has smiled favorably, know something of the shocks of life, the bitter aftertaste of failure, or even the tedium that accompanies the quotidian round. Indeed, even if we have not personally experienced profound tragedy, all of us surely know those who have. For example, we can readily recount stories of the untimely death of a young person, or of the suicide of one who did not seem to fit in, or of potentially productive persons crippled by drugs. We know of children born with debilitating diseases, and of the millions born into obscene poverty, and of the slaughter of millions more. Natural disasters and preventable disease wipe out hundreds of thousands every year, and the death toll from the many wars is so massive as to stagger the imagination. The list goes on and on. And so the nagging questions forces its way into our consciousness: "What does it all come to? Is *this* the meaning of life?"

In fact, it is not only tragedy—unmerited suffering, untimely death, etc.—that presses the question. There is the less dramatic, but inevitable passage of time, with the accompanying disintegration of organisms, as we move inexorably toward the particular death that awaits each of us. All of us who have passed beyond the fresh bloom of youth, having spotted an extra line about the eyes or a bit of gray, and realizing that the body does not respond with the alacrity that it once did, have shuddered at the awareness of our mortality: "Mais où sont les neiges d'antan?"[4] Where, indeed, are the snows of yesteryear? If we are of a mind to put it this way, we might say, with an American philosopher: "Time is the tooth that gnaws; it is the destroyer; we are born only to die and every day brings us nearer death."[5] Actually, of course, this philosopher is only echoing Job who said: "A mortal, born of

---

4. Francois Villon, "Le Grand Testament. Ballade des Dames du Temps Jadis," *Familiar Quotations: A collection of passages, phrases and proverbs traced to their sources in ancient and modern literature. Sixteenth Edition, John Bartlett,* Justin Kaplan, General Editor (Boston: Little, Brown and Co., 1992), 134.

5. John Dewey, "Time and Individuality," *On Experience, Nature, and Freedom* (Indianapolis: The Bobbs-Merrill Co., 1960), 225

THE LAST THINGS

woman, [is but] few of days and full of trouble, comes up like a flower and withers, flees like a shadow and does not last" (Job:14:1–2).

With the utter realization of our transience many are compelled to reflect on the possibility that with death we perish and are obliterated from reality. Certainly, it is not only those who take a short view, or even those few who seem to be constitutionally irreligious, or even those awakened from their slumber by the shock of tragedy, who raise this possibility. Consider the ancient words of Sirach:

> [There are some for whom] there is no memory;
> they have perished as though they had never existed;
> they have become as though they had never been born,
> they and their children after them. (Sirach 44:9)

Consider also the dispiriting stanza of the otherwise powerful, confident hymn, "O God Our Help in Ages Past":

> Time, like an ever-rolling stream, bears all our years away;
> They fly, forgotten, as a dream dies at the opening day.[6]

Now, if the overwhelming realization of the evanescence of existence and the threat of annihilation at death intrudes itself upon all persons—whether by dint of tragedy or by the onset of age—it is just as true that religions (which, as we have seen, do not inevitably try to evade the issue) exist to give meaning to life and to answer the ultimate questions about our whence and our whither, the why and wherefore of life, its origin and goal.

The Christian Message of Hope

Before taking up what I consider to be the most adequate answer to these questions, I want to take notice of an attempt to ground our hope in immortality on supposed empirical evidence. There are some who have claimed to have gained support for a belief in a life after this life from the reports of those who seem to have experienced clinical death and both looked back on the events of this life and, at the same time, glimpsed something of what is there "on the other side." I have no way of evaluating such claims. I have not experienced what they claim to have experienced, and I would not, moreover, know whether these experiences are of something wholly

---

6. Isaac Watts, in *The Hymnal 1982*, #680. The hymn, including the stanza quoted, is a paraphrase of Psalm 90:1–5.

beyond the self and ordinary experiences, or whether they are experiences within the brain much like the common experiences of *déjà vu* or those of night and day dreams or memory. More to the point, however, I can hardly see how claims for a soul's survival of death for a few hours could support anything like the hope for *everlasting* conscious life, the hope for "subjective immortality."[7] As clinically interesting as such reports may be, they are theologically otiose.

Are there, then, any grounds for the "good news" proclaimed by Christianity? It is clear, I believe, that Christianity's message to the world is one of hope. It offers to all persons, everywhere, and no matter what their situation, the hope that their lives are redeemed by God. That is, no matter what tragedy may have befallen them, or how grim their prospects for even the minimal amenities of life, no matter how racked with pain, how blinded by the tears of frustration, no matter that they may be choked by poverty, crippled by disease, shut out of the market place of fair chance by the greedy powers of this world or simply by the passing fortunes of birth, or slaughtered—no matter; Christianity offers to all the hope of salvation. It bears witness to the confidence that our lives are not a passing whiff of insignificance, that they, indeed, have meaning and worth, not simply among the finite few with whom we ordinarily interact, but everlastingly. *Our lives are ultimately significant, because they matter to God.*

This message is compelling, and must be taken seriously. Yet, in taking it seriously, we are bound to reflect on its *meaning* rather than merely hearing the words and assuming that we know what they mean. In fact, it is my guess that most of us forget about the real meaning of the Christian message of hope as we concentrate our attention on the symbols by which that hope gets expressed. What is more, I suspect that this diversion of our attention away from the center to the periphery is often a result of the idolatry that tries to make *us*, rather than God, the center of existence, its be all and end all.

---

7. I use this phrase to convey the conventional view that conscious individual souls survive death forever in an afterlife or heaven. It is used this way by both David Ray Griffin and Schubert Ogden. See, for example, Griffin and Smith, *Primordial Truth and Postmodern Theology*, 4, 25, 130; and, Ogden, *The Reality of God*, 36, 225, 229, 230; and Ogden, "The Meaning of Christian Hope,", 199, 207, 210.

THE LAST THINGS

The Symbols of Resurrection and Immortality

Let us look first, briefly, at the way in which the Christian message of hope has traditionally been expressed. The basic message was expressed in the New Testament and in subsequent Christian literature in terms of two sets of symbols or myths. These symbols were pre-Christian, and they were, in origin and expectation, quite distinct. There were those, on the one hand, that spoke of the resurrection of the body, or of the bodies of all the elect, on the last day. Other symbols expressed belief in the immortality of the soul taken up on the death of the individual.

Originally, expectations of resurrection came out of Persia and, at the time of the writing of the New Testament, were fairly widespread among certain groups of Jews. The beliefs in resurrection, together with various apocalyptic visions of the last times, found an especially fertile soil among a people who had been crushed by the heel of foreign powers for centuries, people who had previously had little concern for life after death, but who were now alienated from life and power in this world. The belief was that this age, presently under the domination of powers at odds with God, would be brought to an abrupt end imminently and that the righteous few would be raised up to meet an emissary of God, "one like a son of man" (Dan 7:13), or, for Christians, the resurrected Christ, often as the Son of Man, who would return in glory (1 Thess 4:13–18; Mark 13), and whose final reign would then commence. When, however, the destruction of this age failed to materialize, the "resurrection of the dead" was pushed back to some distant future "end of time" when all would be judged and the righteous who had died would rise to take on new bodies. The process of "demythologizing" began early.

The belief in the immortality of the soul, on the other hand, was introduced in Greek mythology and speculated about by Greek philosophers, but, at the time of the rise of Christianity, was especially associated with a wide-ranging movement known as "Gnosticism."[8] The Gnostics were thought to have secret knowledge about salvation, and some of their groups whose ideas penetrated the Christian imagination, believed that when a true believer died his or her soul—which had been imprisoned in the body—was immediately released and enabled to ascend into heaven, the divine realm of light.

---

8. See Jonas, *The Gnostic Religion*.

The belief in the "subjective immortality" of the individual soul, released immediately upon the death of its body into a heaven of similar souls where it will it interact endlessly with those souls and with God, has taken over in the popular imagination. The belief in the general resurrection at the end of time has receded somewhat, even though it is still retained in official formulations such as the Nicene Creed where it is said that the risen-ascended Christ "will come again in glory to judge the living and the dead, and his kingdom will have no end" so that "we look for the resurrection of the dead, and the life of the world to come."[9]

Perhaps the two mythologies, with their symbols of resurrected bodies and immortal souls, can be woven together to try to express the hope both for the significance of the individual and the destiny of the whole created order that the specifically Christian form of faith demands. Even so, we must be careful to distinguish the myths from the realities they represent or express. It is a mistake to treat the symbols and myths as themselves pointing to temporal states or observable entities that can be perceived by the senses and that empirical science should try to verify or empirical history attempt to locate. It has long since been established that the point of the biblical myths is, not to give factual information about the ordinary world of things, times, and places, but rather to express our deepest human relationship with ultimate reality.[10]

---

9. "The Nicene Creed," in *The Book of Common Prayer*, 359.

10. It was precisely with respect to eschatological symbols that Reinhold Niebuhr famously said: "It is important to take Biblical symbols seriously but not literally. If they are taken literally the Biblical conception of a dialectical relationship between history and superhistory is imperiled." Reinhold Niebuhr, *The Nature and Destiny of Man*, 50. The best and clearest understanding of the point of myth, however, and what biblical myths intend and why they must, therefore, be "demythologized" is given by Bultmann: "The real point of myth is not to give an objective world picture; what is expressed in it, rather, is how we human beings understand ourselves in our world. Thus, myth does not want to be interpreted in cosmological terms but . . . in existential terms. Myth talks about the power or the powers that we think we experience as the ground and limit of our world and of our action and passion. It talks about these powers in such a way, to be sure, as to bring them within the circle of the familiar world. . . . Myth talks about the unworldly as worldly, the gods as human [Here Bultmann adds a note: "That mode of representation is mythology in which what is unworldly and divine appears as what is worldly and human or what is transcendent appears as what is immanent."]

"What is expressed in myth is the faith that the familiar and disposable world in which we live does not have its ground and aim in itself but that its ground and limit lie beyond all that is familiar and disposable and that this is constantly threatened and controlled by the uncanny powers that are its ground and limit. In unity with this myth also gives expression to the knowledge that we are not lords of ourselves, that we are not only

THE LAST THINGS

This being the case, then, it will be seen that the symbols and myths pertaining to the "last things" have nothing to do with temporal events or with places ("in heaven"). Whenever we entangle ourselves in questions about what is going to happen in the future—whether *my* future immediately following my death or the *collective* future of humanity at some projected date when time comes to an end—we miss the point of the biblical symbols and myths about the last things. They always have to do with the ultimate meaning of existence at *any* moment of time. Christian hope, therefore, is primarily focused on our lives now, that is, with their present relation to God and to God's creation. Hope is only secondarily concerned with the future. To get this point we must be willing to look through the various mythical expressions to their *intention*. As Ogden has said: "Christian hope itself . . . is the criterion for judging the mythology—not the other way around." Therefore, he insists that "the language of hope must be demythologized. It must be interpreted in terms of its own intention to disclose the truth of our own existence in relation to reality as a whole," to which he adds the clarification that "the criterion of our interpretation can only be the specifically Christian understanding of man's relation to God."[11]

The Ground and Object of our Hope: God

As difficult as it may be to keep this point before our eyes, if we do so we will remind ourselves that the ground and object of our hope, as indeed of our faith and our love, is *God*; it is not ourselves, not even humanity generally. It is the eternally existing God, whose boundless love for the world continuously creates and redeems all that we are and do, who is the source and goal of all genuine hope. This is the essential message of good news proclaimed to the world in the life and death of Jesus Christ as disclosing that even the worst cannot annul God's saving love. We may also say that the essential message of the good news is that what is ultimately real and of final worth, and therefore the ground and end of our trust, is not merely the

---

dependent within the familiar world but that we are especially dependent upon the powers that hold sway beyond all that is familiar, and that it is precisely in dependence on them that we can become free from the familiar powers.

"Therefore, the motive for criticizing myth, that is, its objectifying representations, is present in myth itself, insofar as its real intention to talk about a transcendent power to which both we and the world are subject is hampered and obscured by the objectifying character of its assertions." Bultmann, *New Testament and Mythology*, 9–10, 42.

11. Ogden, "The Meaning of Christian Hope," 203.

world or the things of the world, but *God's all-inclusive love for the world*, which love saves and redeems us.

Because we can put our final trust, our ultimate hope, in God's love for all of God's creatures, we are freed from a debilitating preoccupation with ourselves; we are liberated from anxieties about what may or may not occur to us in the future. Thus, we are enabled by God's redemptive love, and our response to it, to care for, nurture, and redeem as much of God's creation as is given into our stewardship. In other words, the object of our hope enables us to "love our neighbors as ourselves," because we can "love God with all of our heart, and all of our soul, and all of our mind." The Christian hope regards each of us as of genuine finite worth, because we are of infinite worth. We are of worth both in the present and everlastingly.

This means that Christian hope, as grounded in the creative and redemptive love of God—both "the Love that moves the sun and the other stars" (Dante) and that "tender care that nothing be lost" (Whitehead)[12]—really has two temporal foci: first and foremost is the here and now; second, however, as the myths of resurrection suggest, is the future.

As I have said, the good news is the liberating news that God's love is for each of us *now*—wherever and however we find ourselves—and it cannot be defeated by our trials, our sufferings, or even our desire to place our final trust in such short-lived things as wealth, beauty, intelligence, or good health. We are never apart from God. Thus every thought we have, every experience we undergo, every deed we perform—for good or for ill—is shared by God's redemptive love. Every occasion of experience is, in fact, taken into, and made a part of, God's ongoing life. This means that, even though we act in the finite world around us or within us, we also and at the same time act on and in God who is our ultimate and immediate environment; we etch our deeds irrevocably into the being of God: "Just as you did it to one of the least of these my brothers and sisters, you did it to me" (Matt 25:40). Whether our thoughts, or deeds, or experiences are as they ought to be, they are redeemed by God's love, and become a part of the ongoing and everlasting life of God. As Hans Jonas, a philosopher with the soul of an artist, puts it:

> In the temporal transactions of the world, whose fleeting now is ever swallowed by the past, an eternal presence grows, its countenance slowly defining itself as it is traced with the joys and

---

12. Dante Alighieri, *The Divine Comedy of Dante*, 303; Whitehead, *Process and Reality*, 346.

sufferings, the triumphs and defeats, of divinity in the experience of time, which thus immortally survive. Not the agents, which must ever pass, but their acts enter into the becoming godhead and indelibly form his never decided image. God's own destiny, his doing and undoing, is at stake in this universe to whose unknowing dealings he committed his substance, and man has become the eminent repository of this supreme and every betrayable trust. In a sense, he holds the fate of deity in his hands.[13]

To be sure, parts of this passage, such as the suggestion that it is possible to bring about God's "undoing," demand clarification. This means that we cause suffering in God even though we could never bring about God's literal demise. (This is acknowledged by also speaking of an "eternal presence" that "grows," and that the "acts" themselves "immortally survive."). But the point is that every deed we do, every thought we have, every moment of our lives is of infinite significance because, as it occurs it is redeemed by God and makes its mark indelibly in the divine experience. Thus, our "acts enter into the becoming godhead and indelibly form his never decided image." Our thoughts and deeds are registered, in every now, in God who continuously redeems them. They are, we may say, *resurrected* into God's life. The focus of our hope is primarily on the present.

Having said this, however, it is clear that the experience of hope inevitably bears within itself an orientation toward the future. The various expressions of hope for resurrection in the New Testament and subsequent Christian literature, and the various representations of the end time and the establishment of God's reign, all point to the future whether imminent or delayed. This means that our expectation is not only that we are significant in the present (God's as well as the world's) but also that we will be significant in the future. It is because God is ever-present yet ongoing, and our lives make their mark in God's ongoing, everlasting life, that our experiences and acts survive into the future. In the words of Jonas our experiences "immortally survive"; our acts "enter into the becoming godhead and indelibly form his never decided image." Whitehead's equally poetic prose holds the present and future in tension:

> For the kingdom of heaven is with us today. . . . What is done in the world is transformed into a reality in heaven, and the reality in heaven passes back into the world. . . . God is the great companion—the fellow-sufferer who understands. We find here

13. Jonas, "Immortality and the Modern Temper," in *The Phenomenon of Life*, 274.

> the final application of the doctrine of objective immortality....
> In this way, the insistent craving is justified—the insistent craving
> that zest for existence be refreshed by the ever-present, unfading
> importance of our immediate actions, which perish and yet live
> for evermore.[14]

The "kingdom of heaven" in which our actions "live for evermore," is the "consequent nature of God."[15] The ground and object of our hope, therefore, is both the present reality of God, and *God's* everlasting future.

A Critique of the Secularist/Atheist Hope

Having now laid out what I take to be the most adequate eschatology, and so the ground of our hope, I owe it to those who reject any belief in God, any idea of God, to consider the implications of their point of view. It is evident that the secular critics of religion, those who deny God and insist that an appeal to any sort of "immortality" is an "illusion," the "opium of the people," nevertheless themselves find reasons to believe that humans can build a world of value before being blotted out; they believe there are grounds for pursuing high ethical ideals even though the final sentence is ... nothingness or "omnipotent matter." So, for instance, Bertrand Russell, in *A Free Man's Worship*, sounds the note of noble optimism in the teeth of "omnipotent Death," when he says: "Brief and powerless is Man's life; on him and all his race the slow, sure doom falls pitiless and dark. Blind to good and evil, reckless of destruction, omnipotent matter rolls on its relentless way; for Man, condemned to day to lose his dearest, tomorrow himself to pass through the gate of darkness, *it remains only to cherish, ere yet the blow falls, the lofty thoughts that ennoble his little day; disdaining the coward terrors of the slave of Fate, to worship at the shrine that his own hands have built* ... the world that his own ideals have fashioned despite the trampling march of unconscious power."[16]

Russell's wholly secular optimism is echoed powerfully in Camus's "absurd hero" in *The Myth of Sisyphus*. There Sisyphus, who has been condemned to the underworld by the gods whom he scorns, to ceaselessly pushing the rock to the top only to have it inevitably roll back again; his "whole being is exerted toward accomplishing nothing." Yet, Camus insists, Sisyphus, the

---

14. Whitehead, *Process and Reality*, 351.
15. Ibid., 350.
16. Russell, *Mysticism and Logic*, 46, 47; my italics.

absurd hero, "is superior to his fate. He is stronger than his rock... I leave Sisyphus at the foot of the mountain! One always finds one's burden again. But Sisyphus teaches the higher fidelity that negates the gods and raises rocks. He too concludes that all is well. The universe henceforth without a master seems to him neither sterile nor futile... The struggle toward the heights is enough to fill a man's heart. One must imagine Sisyphus happy."[17]

The bravado of both Russell and Camus betrays an uneasiness with the implication of their atheism. And, in fact, Camus, in one of his last essays (cited in chapter 1), came clean about this and acknowledged the inadequacy of what was taken to be his previous view:

> The absurd can be considered only as a point of departure.... In any case, how can one limit oneself to the idea that nothing has sense and that we must despair of everything? Without going to the bottom of the matter, one can at least observe that, in the same way that there is no absolute materialism, since merely in order to fashion this word it is already necessary to say that there is in the world something more than matter, there is no total nihilism. From the moment one says that all is nonsense, one expresses something which has sense. Refusing all meaning to the world amounts to abolishing all value judgments.... Anyway, what is the meaning of a literature of despair? Despair is silent.... A literature of despair is a contradiction in terms.[18]

Camus had seen, finally, what Russell and contemporary atheistic ethicists fail to grasp, namely, as Whitehead put it: "Importance, limited to a finite individual occasion, ceases to be important... Importance is derived from the immanence of infinitude in the finite."[19] Or, as we have insisted throughout this work, every experience of every actuality "is a realization of worth, good or bad. It is a value experience. Its basic expression is—Have a care, here is something that matters!" And to be something that matters is to be something of "intrinsic importance for itself, for the others, and for the whole." Moreover, the "whole" is the "infinite whole" of reality. Thus, Whitehead continues, "our sense of the value of the details for the totality dawns upon our consciousness. This is the intuition of holiness, the intuition of the sacred, which is the foundation of all religion."[20] A

---

17. Camus, *The Myth of Sisyphus*, 89, 91.
18. Camus, "The Riddle," 85.
19. Whitehead, *Modes of Thought*, 28.
20. Ibid., 159, 164.

line from one of Whitehead's last public lectures sums it up: "What does haunt our imagination is that the immediate facts of present action pass into permanent significance for the Universe. The insistent notion of Right and Wrong, Achievement and Failure, depends upon this background. Otherwise every activity is merely a passing whiff of insignificance."[21]

Thus, it seems clear that to be anything of worth is to be something that matters infinitely or, what is the same, something that matters *for God*! On the other hand, if everything is destined to be obliterated, then nothing can be said to matter; if all comes to the same thing in the end—nothing—then everything is on a par, which is to say, it matters not a whit. I believe that the courageous proponents of living meaningful and ethical lives without any ultimate reference—that is, while simultaneously holding that our acts, and any possible acts, finally make no difference at all—do not take seriously enough the observation of Qoheleth that "all is vanity," because "time and chance happen to them all" (Eccl 1:2, 9:11).

But let us waive the logical point and grant to the optimistic secular critics of religion that human lives *may* have some meaning when they have no ultimate meaning, or that within an ultimate context of nihilism we can eke out value. Even conceding this brave hope, we should consider that much of our incredibly rich inner lives is simply lost to posterity. A vast amount of the texture of our experience—most of the nuances of our thought, our emotional experiences, and even our physical experiences—is barely perceived by others, and most of the concrete detail of it is missed entirely. What is more, much of this is effaced from conscious memory, and left to die "as a dream dies at the opening day." Large chunks of experience are simply lost. That is, they are lost *if* there is no universal and everlasting memory, *if* there literally is no one unto whom "*all* hearts are open, *all* desires known, and from whom *no* secrets are hid."[22]

---

21. Whitehead, "Immortality," 698.

22. The phrase is, of course, from the Collect for Purity in *The Book of Common Prayer*, 323. Hartshorne, in his essay, "Time, Death, and Everlasting Life," argues persuasively that divine memory as utter omniscience is the only adequate registry of all acts. Having first likened our lives to a book that is continuously written from day one to the final hour, and that can neither be effaced from reality nor written continuously anew in a postmortem state, he says: "Our adequate immortality can only be God's omniscience of us. He to whom all hearts are open remains evermore open to any heart that ever has been apparent to Him. What we once were to Him, less than that we never can be, for otherwise He Himself as knowing us would lose something of His own reality; and this loss of some thing that has been must be final, since, if deity cannot furnish the abiding reality of events, there is, as we have seen, no other way, intelligible to us at least, in

THE LAST THINGS

Take, for example, one's relationship with a parent. I remember my father. Of course, I have a number of cherished memories that illustrate his general character. But who could imagine that I knew his inner life at all intimately? How could I have? I only knew my father at all beginning in his thirty-eighth year. And then I only knew him on a daily basis for about twenty years, and, of course, missed much of his concrete experience during that time. To be sure, my father told me stories of his youth, but how could I share much of that experience which was, by in large, foreign to me? How could a young boy, for that matter, share the experience of a middle-aged father, husband, and worker who was having millions of experiences from which I was, perforce, excluded? How could a young man fathom the experiences of a man in his sixties and seventies who then died? My mother, too, is dead, and my brother and sister are in much the same boat as I. Therefore, so far as the progeny, and other intimates, are concerned much—virtually all—of that rich life is lost, irrevocably lost to a merely finite world. So, in effect, the secular hope for meaning and worth in a world devoid of God is a sham.

What is genuine, however, is the religious hope. The Christian conviction, and that of religions generally, is that the finite future and the survivors in the world are *not* the ultimate repository of anyone's thoughts and deeds. We need not lament, nor even acknowledge, their utter loss. The good news proclaimed by the life and death of Jesus of Nazareth is that God is our ultimate environment, and that God's love that energizes all being also redeems all. Therefore, although others may forget us, or slight us, or ignore us—others may simply fail to share our inner experiences—God neither fails to experience every detail nor lets any slip away. God attends to, loves, cherishes, redeems every detail of every life. Every experience we have, every act we perform, is of everlasting value, because it has its final resting place in God and in God's redemptive love for the world. Thus our hope is for the everlasting significance of our deeds and our experiences—good or bad. In other words, our hope is for their "objective immortality"

---

which it can be furnished. Now the meaning of omniscience is a knowledge which is coextensive with reality, which can be taken as the measure of reality. Hence, if we can never be less than we have been to God, we can in reality never be less than we have been. Omniscience and the in destructibility of every reality are correlative aspects of one truth. Death cannot mean the destruction or even the fading, of the book of one's life; it can mean only the fixing of its concluding page. Death writes 'The End' upon the last page, but nothing further happens to the book, by way of either addition or subtraction." *The Logic of Perfection*, 252–53.

in the immortal life of God and, insofar as God chooses to make them relevant, in the lives of subsequent occasions of the world.

A Critique of the Hope for Subjective Immortality

I have contended that the secularist/atheist lacks any solid ground for pursuing ethical ideals, because the position amounts to "abolishing all value judgments" and amounts to the confession that all our acts and experiences are but a "passing whiff of insignificance." At the same time I have tried to show that an adequate eschatology can only be one that affirms our "objective immortality" in God who alone abides.

It remains to consider the hope that I have identified as the hope for "subjective immortality." Does our faith demand the additional belief that when we die we do not really die, but that our souls are kept intact as conscious, ongoing, spiritual subjects who enjoy life everlasting in the presence of God? When we say that God "keeps us as the apple of his eye," must we mean that we go to heaven as discrete, eternal yet living souls who have ever new relationships with other souls, many of whom have "gone before," and with God? This seems to be the conventional view of an afterlife in heaven. But is it demanded by faith or the Bible or by a "reasonable, holy, and living" worship of God? I do not think so. To be sure the specific character of any ultimate existence, whether ours or God's, must remain a mystery to finite minds. And so, in the nature of the case, no definitive answer to this question can be given. Even so, there is no reason to suppose that the belief in God and in (conscious human) immortality are inextricably bound together. I do not believe that an allegiance to the Christian hope in God's redemptive love demands the express belief that discrete, conscious individuals will survive immortally in an afterlife, having what I have called "subjective immortality." The conventional idea of our subjective immortality, however, is set about with several attitudes and ideas that reinforce it. Perhaps, if we bring these to the surface and shed some light on them, the hold they have on us will diminish.

First and foremost, I believe, is what I can only call a psychological need for security and a longing to be justified. Because suffering, failure, and death make us uncomfortable, we long to be at peace and, perhaps, to have the opportunity to rectify old mistakes and to have ever-new relationships. The prospect of being cut short by death seems just too unsettling for many of us to contemplate.

THE LAST THINGS

But is it? I confess that the thought of my own death has not been disquieting to me. Like others, to be sure, I do not enjoy the thought of the pain that sometimes precedes death. Also like others, I would love to have my wits about me and be able to maintain a relatively sound body until I die. Of course, anyone lucky enough to live past his or her seventies can expect diminished powers. And many can expect debilitating end-of-life diseases. But is death itself a threat? No. I recall reading Plato's *Apology* in my late teens and being persuaded then by Socrates's reasons "to hope that death is a good." He suggested two possible scenarios to follow death, the second of which anticipated our own conventional view that when we pass beyond death we will take up and enjoy relations with those who have preceded us. As Socrates says, "What would not a man give if he might converse with Orpheus and Musaeus and Hesiod and Homer . . . or Odysseus or Sisyphus, or numberless others, men and women too! What infinite delight would there be in conversing with them and asking them questions!" This scenario seemed to me to be very like the conventional view, only with no God to deal with, and it is, I suspect, what many still hope for. But I did not then find it particularly reassuring, nor do I now.

It was, however, the first scenario that struck me then as comforting, and has stuck with me since: Perhaps "death is a state of nothingness and utter unconsciousness," Socrates says. "If you suppose that there is no consciousness, but a sleep like the sleep of him who is undisturbed even by dreams, death will be an unspeakable gain. For if a person were to select the night in which his sleep was undisturbed even by dreams . . . if death be of such a nature, I say that to die is a gain; for eternity is then only a single night."[23] As I say, the realization that death could take us into sheer unconsciousness like that of a dreamless sleep appealed to me as not at all threatening. Only I have the deeper conviction that I will have been something that matters—for good and for ill—to God who alone abides. There is really no psychological need for postmortem rewards and punishments nor for the consolation of a continuing, conscious, interactive life.

Another sentiment, however, that induces many to hope for our subjective survival of death in an afterlife is less preoccupied with self. It is far more other-regarding and attuned to issues of justice. It is driven by a deep concern that wrongs be righted, and it well knows that the world has produced so very many whose lives were neither long nor happy; "they have perished as though they had never existed," or else, through no fault of

---

23. Plato, *Apology, Crito, Phaedo, Symposium, Republic*, 59–60.

their own and often in wretched circumstances, they have been snuffed out prematurely. As one student put it to me: "I cannot shake off the anger and the anguish I feel when I think of the *children* who were killed in the Holocaust or those slaughtered in the genocides of Rwanda and Darfur; and I cannot believe that a loving and just God would allow such unjustifiable suffering to go unredeemed." Indeed, as we have already remarked, there are many millions who have undergone immeasurable suffering in a short life and have met untimely deaths. It is very natural for devout and sensitive believers to hope for some rectification of injustices in an afterlife. But it is equally natural for sensitive atheists to reply sharply that no God "worth his salt" would allow such unmerited suffering to occur in the first place. Thus many atheists believe that the existence of atrocities in this world disproves the existence of God.[24]

We can sympathize with the sentiments of both the sensitive believer and the indignant atheist. Yet they are misdirected because they are misconceived. The desire of the believer for an afterlife where wrongs are righted, as well as that of the atheist for a world where no evil occurs or else is reduced so that bad things do *not* happen to good people, rests upon an idea of God and of divine power that is childish, non-biblical, and not rational.

I do not mean to be flippant by asserting that the expectations of the subjective immortalist and the atheist, in their desire that God inevitably make things right, are "childish," but they remind me of nothing so much as the sentiment of the child in A. A. Milne's poem, "If I Were King": "I often wish I were a King, and then I could do anything . . . I think, if I were King of Greece, I'd push things off the mantelpiece . . . If I were King of Timbuctoo, I'd think of lovely things to do. If I were King of anything, I'd tell the soldiers, 'I'm the King!'"[25] Children often mistakenly imagine that great power is the ability to remove obstacles, to change results, and to manipulate others; in short, to "do anything."

---

24. This is the gravamen of Sam Harris's argument in his little book, *Letter to a Christian Nation*. See, for instance, pages 51–55, where he claims that "the entirety of atheism is contained in" the response to the many atrocities the world experiences: "An atheist is a person who believes that the murder of a single little girl—even once in a million years—casts doubt upon the idea of a benevolent God . . . if God exists, either He can do nothing to stop the most egregious calamities, or He does not care to. God, therefore, is either impotent or evil. . . . There is another possibility, of course, and it is both the most reasonable and least odious: the biblical god is a fiction."

25. Milne, *The World of Christopher Robin*, 111.

THE LAST THINGS

Likewise, the idea is non-biblical. As we saw in chapter 3 the essential biblical portrait of God is not that of an absolute determiner of all outcomes. The God of the Bible, who is supremely worthy of worship, is the God of pure unbounded love, the personal whole of reality. "Divine love," we saw, "is not the ability to act unilaterally for our good, but the inexhaustible compassion that understands all because it is affected by all and suffers with all." To long for a world, either here or hereafter, where evil can be eradicated or where lives, once miserable and then cut short, can be remade anew, is to presuppose a God at odds with the biblical God. It is better to accept the fact that God knows, loves, and redeems our lives "just as [they are] without one plea."

The irrationality of the idea has to do mainly with the idea of "omnipotence" that it presupposes: the power to "do anything" that God might wish, to wholly determine the outcome of any event. In the first place, as Aquinas said, "nothing that implies a contradiction falls under the scope of God's omnipotence,"[26] and changing or eliminating the past, which is stubborn fact, or making the free decision of another for it, or postponing the death of mortals indefinitely, may be seen as logical impossibilities and so contradictions. Moreover, as Hartshorne often maintained, the notion of one being in a universe of finite beings having a monopoly of power is a non-idea and a bad one at that. For instance, he says: "For X to have a power to prevent anything undesirable from occurring is for X to have a monopoly on decision-making. But this monopoly is itself the most undesirable thing imaginable; or rather *it is the unimaginable and indeed inconceivable absolutizing of an undesirable direction of thought.* Monopoly of decision-making is in principle undesirable."[27]

---

26. *Summa Theologica*, I, Q. 25, a.4 (p. 265).

27. Hartshorne, "A New Look at the Problem of Evil," 202. With respect to the "problem of evil" Hartshorne says (207–8): "(a) it is a pseudoproblem due to a pseudoconcept of omnipotence or divine power; evil springs from creaturely freedom, and without such freedom there could be no world at all; (b) creaturely freedom capable of producing evil, at least in the form of suffering, is universal to the creation, not confined to man or rational animals or even to animals; (c) God's supremacy consists, not in his making the creatures' decisions for them, but in his setting abstract limits of law to creaturely decisions, and in his ideally free evaluations of the results so that they acquire permanent meaning; finally, (d) God shares in all suffering since he cherishes all creatures, so that he may be seen as the ideal companion in sorrow as well as joy. God would be masochistic as well as sadistic if it were true that he deliberately caused us to suffer. But he is neither, for no concrete evil is divinely decided, whether as punishment, means of spiritual education, or in view of any other end. God sets the creatures free, within limits, because there is no other way to have creatures or any world. The risks of freedom are inseparable

I also think it is unreasonable to suppose that righting wrongs in an afterlife would mitigate the original evils or change the fact that they occurred in the first place. Nor can a postmortem system of rewards and punishments correct anything or recompense us for the ills we have suffered. If a child has suffered and died the child has suffered and died, and God can share its suffering and love it for what it is, but God cannot revise the past out of existence.

Reasonable theists have a wholly different understanding of divine power. It is essentially the power of love: the power to create by enabling the free decisions of others within a conditioned setting; the power to redeem all that has been done; the power to suffer with the creatures in their suffering; and the power to embrace all this everlastingly.

Still, no matter how unreasonable and psychologically immature belief in our subjective immortality might be, when all is said and done does not the Scripture insist that "souls go to heaven" or that we are resurrected into an afterlife, "the life of the world to come"? And doesn't this trump all appeal to psychology and reason?[28] Let us examine this claim.

In fact, there are precious few references in the Bible to souls going to heaven. The one really good passage about souls and God is to be found in the Wisdom of Solomon: "But the souls of the righteous are in the hand of God, and no torment will ever touch them . . . Their hope is full of immortality" (Wis 3:1, 4). This passage ought, properly, to be understood as having to do with our objective immortality in God.

Many of the references to "heaven" in the New Testament are to be found in Matthew where "the kingdom of heaven" is synonymous with "the reign or the rule of God," which refers to God's rule in this world. Even

---

from freedom, and the price of its opportunities. Without freedom there could be nothing, whether good or evil."

28. We are much too ready to assert that "the Bible says . . ." Consider, for instance, the running "church signs" debate that is being passed around by email: *A Catholic Church*: "All dogs go to heaven." *A Presbyterian Church* (across the street): "Only humans go to heaven. Read the Bible" *Catholic*: "God loves all his creations, dogs included." *Presbyterian*: "Dogs don't have souls. This is not open to debate." *Catholic*: "Catholic dogs go to heaven. Presbyterian dogs can talk to their pastor." *Presbyterian*: "Converting to Catholicism does not magically grant your dog a soul." *Catholic*: "Free dog souls with conversion." *Presbyterian*: "Dogs are animals. There aren't any rocks in heaven either." *Catholic*: "All rocks go to Heaven." Of course, the Catholics have the better sense of humor here. And, if they are willing to demythologize "going to heaven" to mean being embraced everlastingly by God, the Catholics have the better of it. But if they both take heaven literally as an afterlife where conscious souls go to have an extended, developing life, both are demanding "subjective immortality," which the Bible may not demand.

THE LAST THINGS

such passages as that at the end of the Beatitudes, "Rejoice and be glad, for your reward is great in heaven" (Matt 5:12), can and should be read as the persecuted having mattered to God who suffers and yet rejoices with them who have their objective immortality in God. When, in Mark, Jesus, in an exchange with the Sadducees about the resurrection, says, "When they rise from the dead they neither marry nor are given in marriage, but are like angels in heaven" (Mark 12:25), it seems clear that he is dismissing the notion of an afterlife where life goes on much as in this world; when we rise from the dead we are with God. I believe that all talk of heaven can, and must be, demythologized. As was said earlier the language of hope must be interpreted in terms of its intention to symbolize our relation to God; we do not judge the meaning of hope by a literal rendering of the mythological symbols.

This is equally the case with the many references of "resurrection" in the New Testament. For instance, Paul's famous assertion—"If there is no resurrection of the dead, then Christ has not been raised; and if Christ has not been raised, then our proclamation has been in vain and your faith has been in vain" (1 Cor 15:13–14)—is followed by an elaborate argument in which he lays bare its meaning: "Christ has been raised from the dead, the first fruits of those who have died . . . For he must reign until he has put all his enemies under his feet. The last enemy to be destroyed is death . . . When all things are subjected to him, then the Son himself will also be subjected to the one who put all things in subjection under him, so that God may be all in all" (15:20, 25–26, 28). This is clearly intended to show that faith in resurrection is faith in God, who is all and in all. Paul even tries to head off a literal understanding of the resurrection of the dead when he says: "What is sown is perishable, what is raised is imperishable. For it is sown in dishonor, it is raised in glory. It is sown in weakness, it is raised in power. It is sown a physical body, it is raised a spiritual body" (15:42–44).

If, then, there are no good psychological, rational, or biblical grounds for construing our hope in terms of our subjective immortality, rather than as our objective immortality in God, there is, at least, one good reason to reject it. And that reason is theological.

It seems that such a belief, however disguised or however well-intentioned, stems from an idolatrous effort to substitute our *own* ultimacy, in the form of our enjoyment of everlasting conscious life, for that which is the *true* ultimate, namely, God. In addition to implying that God must repay us for our suffering and reward us for the good we have done, the hope for our own subjective immortality seems to arise out of what is typically called "original sin." That is to say, this hope expresses the deep human desire to "be like God" (Gen 3:5) insofar as it expresses the hope that we may escape our finitude and become immortal. Reinhold Niebuhr put it bluntly: "Man is mortal. That is his fate. Man pretends not to be mortal. That is his sin."[29] Christianity has consistently refused to endorse the belief in the soul's *pre*-existence for the reason that such a belief represents the attempt to usurp the place of deity. It ought, for the same reason, to reject the idea of our continued *post*-existence as centered, self-conscious selves. Ogden put it well when he said that our sin "[i]s precisely [the] refusal to acknowledge [our] dependence on God . . . [so that our] faith takes the inauthentic form that Scripture speaks of as idolatry—that is, the setting up of something alongside of God's love as alone justifying [our] life by finally making it worth living . . . It is this very refusal to live, finally, solely from God's love for us that I find involved in the setting up of our own subjective immortality alongside of our objective immortality in God."[30] I think this is decisive.

In addition, however, a reason for calling into question the hope for subjective immortality is the ethical objection brought forth by secular critics of Christianity from the time of Feuerbach and Marx to the present: the extreme focus on the afterlife has the real effect of depriving this life—our thought, our efforts for justice—of any genuine value. Precisely because our hope has been focused on a perfect life after this one, where "they shall hunger no more neither thirst anymore . . . and God will wipe away every tear from their eyes" (Rev 7:16, 17, citing various passages from the Hebrew Bible), we have forged an "unholy alliance" with forces for exploitation and oppression of the poor and marginalized. This is not a charge that can be brought against the belief in our objective immortality.[31]

---

29. Reinhold Niebuhr, *Beyond Tragedy*, 28.

30. Ogden, "The Meaning of Christian Hope," 209.

31. So Ogden argues ("The Meaning of Christian Hope," 210–11): "By focusing our ultimate hope on our subjective existence beyond death, Christianity appears to many of our contemporaries to belittle the urgent problems of a humanity struggling for greater justice and enlightenment and to provide at least a negative sanction for the social and political status quo. And this appears all the more certain to them because, with its virtual abandonment of apocalypticism as expressing a truly collective hope, much of modern Christianity has, in fact, focused man's ultimate expectations on the existence beyond death of the individual persons. Thus it has been widely taught in modern Churches that all that finally counts is the other-worldly salvation of individuals, with the result that efforts for the fulfillment and humanization of this world have been deprived of any ultimate significance."

THE LAST THINGS

An Affirmation of the Hope for our Objective Immortality

To call subjective immortality into question is in no way to abandon hope. To live in the faith that all our lives—all experiences, deeds, and thoughts—are something that matters, are registered unfailingly in God's everlasting life where they are redeemed and made of abiding worth, is to be perfectly hopeful. Paul's resurrection hope is expressed profoundly in Romans: "If God is for us, who is against us? He who did not withhold his own Son, but gave him up for us all, will he not with him also give us everything else? . . . It is God who justifies. Who is to condemn? . . . Who will separate us from the love of Christ? Will hardship, or distress, or persecution, or famine, or nakedness or peril, or sword? . . . No, in all these things we are more than conquerors through him who loved us. For I am convinced that neither death, nor life, nor angels, nor rulers, nor things present, nor things to come, nor powers, nor height, nor depth, nor anything else in all creation, will be able to separate us from the love of God in Christ Jesus our Lord" (Rom 8:31–39). Again Paul says: "If we live we live unto the Lord, and if we die we die unto the Lord, so then, whether we live or whether we die, we are the Lord's" (14:8).

Conclusion

This last chapter brings the work to a close and tries to express summarily the point of view running through it. I can think of no better summary of the whole than the opening of this chapter:

> [T]he doctrine of the 'last things' is really but an elaboration of our first principle, namely, that we live as humans at all only in the abiding confidence that we, and all creatures, are finally 'something that matters.' The Christian faith, which may be said to be a sharper, more explicit, form of this common faith of humanity, holds that all creatures make a difference not only to our fellow beings which constitute our finite environment but to God revealed by Jesus Christ as the Father whose pure unbounded love redeems 'all creatures great and small.' God is the all-inclusive One 'unto whom all hearts are open, all desires known, and from whom no secrets are hid.' Thus, the Christian hope is in the love of God that redeems and makes of everlasting value all finite acts and experiences. Nothing that occurs is either ignored or swept away; it is

treasured for what it is and can be, and is saved for evermore in the ongoing life of God. In God alone there is no lapse of memory, and nothing is lost or misinterpreted; in God alone the full ramifications of all deeds are felt and fully appreciated. Only in the life of God can any experience or occasion be valued adequately and with full understanding, full compassion. Only as it is 'objectively immortal' in God can any occasion, finally, be said to be 'something that matters.'

This faith and its hope, we have seen, is far more firmly grounded, reasonable, and ethical than that of either atheistic secularism or traditional Christian belief. The former is not as rational as its proponents believe, and it has no grounds for faith and hope; also, it abolishes all value judgments, for all comes to nothing in the end. The latter projects an idea of God that is non-biblical, nonsensical, and for whom nothing in this world could possibly make a difference; it is a God for whom we are something that does *not* matter. By contrast, I have taken the biblical image of God seriously, and have shown it to be reasonable and the ground of a reasonable and compassionate ethics. To worship God is to love God with all of our being and to love those whom God loves—all creatures great and small—unreservedly. This is the God for whom all are something that matters. Here, I believe, we are at the heart of the Christian proclamation of good news.

WORKS CITED

Allport, Gordon. *The Individual and His Religion.* New York: Macmillan, 1967.
Anselm. *St. Anselm: Proslogium; Monologium; An Appendix in Behalf of the Fool by Gaunilon; and Cur Deus Homo.* Translated by Sidney Norton Deane. LaSalle, IL: Open Court, 1958.
Aquinas, Thomas. *Basic Writings of Saint Thomas Aquinas.* Edited and Annotated, with an Introduction by Anton. C. Pegis. New York: Random House, 1945.
Bonhoeffer, Dietrich. *Letters and Papers from Prison.* Enlarged ed. Edited by Eberhard Bethge. London: SCM, 1974.
The Book of Common Prayer: According to the use of The Episcopal Church. New York: Church Pension Fund, 1986.
Brooke, Rupert. "The Soldier." In *Norton Anthology of English Literature*, edited by M. H. Abrams, 2:1827. 6th ed. New York: W.W. Norton, 1993.
Bultmann, Rudolf. *New Testament and Mythology and Other Basic Writings.* Edited and translated by Schubert M. Ogden. Philadelphia: Fortress, 1984.
Camus, Albert. *The Myth of Sisyphus and Other Essays.* New York: Vintage, 1955.
———. "The Riddle." *Atlantic Monthly* 211 (1963) 83–85.
Carroll James. *Constantine's Sword: The Church and the Jews.* New York: Houghton Mifflin, 2001.
Carroll, Lewis. *The Annotated Alice: Alice's Adventures in Wonderland and Through the Looking Glass.* Introduction and Notes by Martin Gardner. New York: Book Craftsmen, 1960.
Cobb, John B., Jr. *God and the World.* Eugene OR: Wipf and Stock, 1998.
Cook, Michael. "The New Testament: Confronting Its Impact on Jewish-Christian Relations." *Introduction to Jewish-Christian Relations.* Edited by Michael Shermis and Arthur E. Zannoni. New York: Paulist, 1991.
Cromwell, Oliver. "Letter to the General Assembly of the Church of Scotland." August, 3 1650. Cited in Wikiquotes. www.cromwell.argonet.co.uk (accessed November 9, 2015.
Dante Alighieri. *The Divine Comedy of Dante Alighieri: Paradiso.* A Verse Translation with Introduction by Allen Mandelbaum. New York: Bantam, 1984.
Darwin, Charles. *The Origin of Species: By Means of Natural Selection of the Preservation of Favoured Races in the Struggle for Life.* Introduced by Sir Julian Huxley. New York: Signet Classics, 2003.

WORKS CITED

Dawkins, Richard. *The God Delusion*. New York: Houghton Mifflin, 2006.

Dennett, Daniel C. *Breaking the Spell; Religion as a Natural Phenomenon*. New York: Penguin, 2007.

Dewey, John. *On Experience, Nature, and Freedom: Representative Selections*. Edited with an Introduction by Richard J. Bernstein. Indianapolis: Bobbs-Merrill, 1960.

Epp, Eldon. "Anti-Semitism and the Popularity of the Fourth Gospel." *Central Conference of American Rabbi's Journal* Fall (1975) 35–53.

Findlay, J. N. "Can God's Existence Be Disproved?" *New Essays in Philosophical Theology*, edited by Antony Flew and Alasdair MacIntyre, 47–56. London: SCM, 1955.

Flew, Antony. *There Is a God: How the World's Most Notorious Atheist Changed His Mind*. New York: Harper Collins, 2007.

Freud, Sigmund. *The Future of an Illusion*. Translated and edited by James Strachey, with a biographical Introduction by Peter Gay. New York: Norton, 1961.

Fromm, Erich. *The Art of Loving*. New York: Harper & Row, 1956.

———. *Man For Himself: An Inquiry into the Psychology of Religion*. Greenwich CT: Fawcett, 1967.

Geertz, Clifford. *The Interpretation of Cultures: Selected Essays*. New York: Basic, 1973.

Gilkey, Langdon. *Creationism on Trial: Evolution and God at Little Rock*. Minneapolis: Winston, 1985.

Griffin, David Ray, and Huston Smith. *Primordial Truth and Postmodern Theology*. Albany: State University of New York Press, 1989.

Harris, Sam. *Letter to a Christian Nation*. New York: Knopf, 2006. "Afterword to the Vintage Book Edition." 2008.

Harris, Stephen L. *The New Testament: A Student's Introduction*. 2nd ed. Mountain View, CA: Mayfield, 1995.

Hartshorne, Charles. *Anselm's Discovery: A Re-Examination of the Ontological Proof for God's Existence*. LaSalle, IL: Open Court, 1965.

———. *Creative Synthesis and Philosophic Method*. LaSalle, IL: Open Court, 1970.

———. *Insights and Oversights of the Great Thinkers: An Evaluation of Western Philosophy*. Albany: State University of New York Press, 1983.

———. *The Logic of Perfection*. LaSalle, IL: Open Court, 1962.

———. "A New Look at the Problem of Evil." In *Current Philosophical Issues: Essays in Honor of Curt John Ducasse*, edited by Frederick C. Dommeyer, 201–12. Springfield, IL: Thomas, 1966.

———. *Reality as Social Process: Studies in Metaphysics and Religion*. Boston: Beacon, 1953.

Hartshorne, Charles, and William L. Reese, eds. *Philosophers Speak of God*. Chicago: University of Chicago Press, 1953.

Henry, Patrick. "Give Me Liberty or Give Me Death." March 23, 1775. http.//libertyonline.hypermail.com/henry-liberty.html (accessed November 11, 2015).

Hick, John, and Arthur McGill, eds. *The Many-Faced Argument: Recent Studies on the Ontological Argument for the Existence of God*. New York: Macmillan, 1967.

Hitchens, Christopher. *God is Not Great: How Religion Poisons Everything*. New York: Twelve, 2007.

The Hymnal 1982. New York: Church Hymnal, 1982.

James, William. *Some Problems of Philosophy: A Beginning of an Introduction to Philosophy*. New York: Longmans, Green, 1911.

WORKS CITED

———. *The Will to Believe and Other Essays in Popular Philosophy and Human Immortality: Two Supposed Objections to the Doctrine.* New York: Dover, 1956.

Jefferson, Thomas. *The Declaration of Independence: In Congress, July 4, 1776. The unanimous Declaration of the thirteen united States of America.* Reprinted in *The U.S. Constitution: And Fascinating Facts About it,* Seventh Edition, 59–63. Supplemental text by Terry L. Jordan. Naperville, IL: Oak Hill, 2008.

Jonas, Hans. *The Gnostic Religion: The Message of an Alien God and the Beginning of Christianity.* Boston: Beacon, 1958.

———. *The Phenomenon of Life: Toward a Philosophy of Biology.* New York: Harper & Row, 1966.

Kant, Immanuel. *Critique of Pure Reason.* Translated by Norman Kemp Smith. New York: Macmillan, 1929.

Kingsley, Charles. *The Water Babies: A Fairy Tale for a Land Baby.* New York: Digireads, 2011.

Lane, Tony. *Harper's Concise Book of Christian Faith.* San Francisco: Harper & Row, 1984.

Luther, Martin. *Three Treatises.* Philadelphia: Fortress, 1970.

Malcolm, Norman. "Anselm's Ontological Arguments." In *The Ontological Argument from St. Anselm to Contemporary Philosophers,* edited by Alvin Plantinga, 136–59. Garden City, NY: Doubleday, 1965.

Marx, Karl. *Basic Writings on Politics and Philosophy: Karl Marx and Friedrich Engels.* Edited by Lewis S. Feuer. Garden City, NY: Doubleday, 1958.

Mason, David R. *Something That Matters: A Theology for Critical Believers.* Santa Barbara CA: Praeger, 2011.

Mason, George. *The Virginia Declaration of Rights.* 1776. In *The Papers of George Mason, 1725–1792,* edited by Robert A. Rutland, 1:283–89. Chapel Hill: University of North Carolina Press, 1970.

May, Rollo. *Love and Will.* New York: Dell, 1969.

McGrath, Alister. *The Twilight of Atheism: The Rise and Fall of Disbelief in the Modern World.* New York: Doubleday, 2004.

McGrath, Alister, and Joanna Collicut McGrath. *The Dawkins Delusion? Atheist Fundamentalism and the Denial of the Divine.* Downers Grove, IL: Intervarsity, 2007.

Miller, John. *The Irony of Christianity.* Cleveland: Institute for Religion in the World, 2002.

Milne, A. A. *The World of Christopher Robin: The Complete When We Were Very Young and Now We Are Six.* With decorations and illustrations by E. H. Shepard. New York: Dutton, 1958.

Niebuhr, H. Richard. *The Meaning of Revelation.* New York: Macmillan, 1962.

Niebuhr, Reinhold. *Beyond Tragedy: Essays on the Christian Interpretation of History.* New York: Scribner's Sons, 1937.

———. *The Nature and Destiny of Man.* Vol. 2, *Human Destiny.* New York: Scribner's Sons, 1943.

Ogden, Schubert M. "The Meaning of Christian Hope." In *Religious Experience and Process Theology: The Pastoral Implications of a Major Modern Movement,* edited by Harry James Cargas and Bernard Lee, 195–212. New York: Paulist, 1976.

———. *The Reality of God and other Essays.* New York: Harper & Row, 1966.

Paine, Thomas. *The American Crisis.* Dec. 23, 1776. The American Crisis: From Revolution to Reconstruction and beyond. http://www.let.rug.nl/usa/documents/1776-1785/thomas-paine-american-crisis/ (accessed November 11, 2015).

WORKS CITED

Perry, Ralph Barton. *The Thought and Character of William James: As Revealed in Unpublished Correspondence and Notes, Together with His Published Writings*. Vol II, *Philosophy and Psychology*. Boston: Little, Brown, 1935.

Pike, Nelson, ed. *God and Evil: Readings on the Theological Problem of Evil*. Englewood Cliffs, NJ: Prentice Hall, 1964.

Plato. *Apology, Crito, Phaedo, Symposium, Republic*. Edited with Introduction by Louise Ropes Loomis. Translated by B. Jowett. New York: Black, 1942.

———. *Plato's Cosmology: The Timaeus of Plato*. Translated with a running commentary by Francis MacDonald Cornford. New York: Liberal Arts, 1957.

Pope, Alexander. *An Essay on Man: Epistle I*. The Poetry Foundation. www.poetryfoundation.org (accessed November 12, 2014).

Price, Lucien. *Dialogues of Alfred North Whitehead*. Boston: Little, Brown, 1954.

Russell, Bertrand. *Mysticism and Logic: And other Essays*. Totowa, NJ: Barnes and Noble, 1981.

Sanders, John. *The God Who Risks: A Theology of Providence*. Downers Grove, IL: Intervarsity, 1998.

Santayana, George. *Scepticism and Animal Faith*. New York: Dover, 1955.

Steinberg, Milton. *Basic Judaism*. Orlando: Harcourt Brace, 1975.

Tillich, Paul. *Dynamics of Faith*. New York: Harper & Bros., 1957.

Tracy, David. *Blessed Rage for Order: The New Pluralism in Theology*. New York: Seabury, 1975.

Wallis, Jim. *God's Politics: Why the Right Gets It Wrong and the Left Doesn't Get It*. New York: HarperCollins, 2005.

Whichcote, Benjamin. *Moral and Religious Aphorisms: Wherein are contained, many doctrines of truth; and rules of practice; . . .* Reproduction from British Library. Gale ECCO Print Edition. Norwich, 1703.

Whitehead, Alfred North. *Adventures of Ideas*. New York: Macmillan, 1933.

———. *The Concept of Nature*. Cambridge: Cambridge University Press, 1964.

———. "Immortality." *The Philosophy of Alfred North Whitehead*. Edited by Paul Arthur Schillp. New York: Tudor, 1941.

———. *Modes of Thought*. Cambridge: Cambridge University Press, 1956.

———. *Process and Reality: An Essay in Cosmology*. Corrected Edition edited by David Ray Griffin and Donald W. Sherburne. New York: Free, 1978.

———. *Religion in the Making*. New York: Macmillan, 1926.

———. *Science and the Modern World*. New York: Macmillan, 1925.

Wright, Robert. *The Evolution of God*. New York: Little, Brown, 2009.

www.ingramcontent.com/pod-product-compliance
Lightning Source LLC
Chambersburg PA
CBHW071231170426
43191CB00032B/1319